If I Die Thursday

John Clinton Gray

If I Die Thursday
© 2016 by John Clinton Gray
ISBN-13: 9780986285363
ISBN-10: 0986285366

GRAY MATTER IMPRINT EDITION

Library of Congress Cataloging-in-Publication Data

Gray, John Clinton
If I Die Thursday, life stories / John Clinton Gray
    Short Story, Essay, Memoir
    ISBN 978-0-9862853-6-3.
    1. Short Stories 2. Essays 3. Memoir

Cover and interior graphics by Amanda Woloshyn of Amanda Woloshyn Marketing & Creative Communications. amanda@awmd.ca

Also by John Clinton Gray: *Gift of Seeds* (2012)

Published by Gray Matter Imprints™, division of Gray Matter Consultants LLC, P.O. Box 50278, Irvine, CA 92619

10 9 8 7 6 5 4 3 2 1

Printed in the United States of America

Gray Matter accepts queries by mail only at:
    Gray Matter Imprints
    P.O. Box 50278
    Irvine, CA 92619
    ISBN: 0986285366

John Clinton Gray's anecdotal stories are always insightful, humorous, and poignant. I recommend them heartily as a good read that is both delightful fun and imaginatively thought-provoking. His vignettes are uncluttered, clear, and hit the mark each time. See the world through John's eyes for the adventure that life is—a profound and wondrous journey that emphasizes the endearing uniqueness of people.

— Larry Krantz, M.D., author of *Strange Miracles* and *Dreams of Atlantis*

John Gray sees the world from a different perspective than most of us. That's why I enjoy reading his stories so much.

The tales themselves appear to be simple observations of daily life, served up in easy-to-digest portions, but inside each is a gift—an insight begging to be grasped. For most of us, such insights come around on rare occasions, and too often we file them away for contemplation later. That won't happen here. His narratives draw us gently to a deeper heart level, where we can pause and reflect. I like that.

Sometimes his stories evoke feelings of joy, jubilation even. Sometimes the feelings are more somber. Regardless, John's well-crafted tales deftly reveal a world always full of wonder and humanity, and I enjoy lingering there with him. I can hardly wait to read more.

— Terry Oftedal, author of *The Story of Sunseed, And Other True Adventures*

A remarkable collection of evocative essays and short stories, *If I Die Thursday* draws us through multiple layers of human experience. Gray's descriptions reconnected me in palpable ways with familiar worlds of childhood, humor, and a perceptive view of life on Earth. "Horrors" reminds us how childhood experiences can unexpectedly resurface. "If I Die Thursday" presents moving insights about human nature, autumnal transitions, and mortality. And "To the Last Bite" delivers delicious puns deep-fried in a snappy corndog batter.

Deeply moving, and a joy to read!

— Peggy Gretsch, children's author/composer, *George Washington and The Cherry Tree* and *The Talented Turkeys of Tillamook* (Marlypeg Music)

Si Yo Muriera el Jueves. Titulo muy sugerente, a través del cual John, mi querido amigo del alma, nos relata con su muy particular humor, su propia manera de experimentar su muerte, en donde plasma de una manera muy simple, pero profunda, su visión del cielo.... Es un libro revelador y lleno de mensajes de hermandad y comunidad. Definitivamente un libro inspirador, que te llenara de esperanza y amor.

— Malena Carrión, autora de *Las Huellas de un Ángel* y *El Grial Interior*

John Clinton Gray has once again given us a collection of essays and stories that delight. Have you ever thought about knowing the actual date for your death? Ever wonder how many people in the world have the same name as yours?

Gray can take everyday ideas and experiences and transmute them into entertaining and, often, profoundly thought-provoking essays. Get comfortable in an easy chair with a glass of wine and let these stories transport you. They made me laugh, cry, and wonder about important things.

— Janet Simcic, author of The *Man at the Realto Bridge* and *The Man at the Caffe' Farnese*

To all who remember

Contents

Best-Selling Arthur

Tucked inside the "Happy Anniversary" card was a gift certificate for dance lessons. At first it struck Pamela and me as a little quirky-funny, but then so is the friend who gave it to us. Dancing? We slowly warmed to the idea. After calling to set a start date, we were eager.

The time came, a rainy evening. We followed our GPS to the Arthur Murray Dance Studio, scampered across the parking lot into its glowing interior, and presented our certificate.

We were there to enjoy our Introductory Package and maybe learn a few dance basics. We didn't know it then, but the "intro special" is designed to lead new students to a Foundation Program—a longer series of private dance lessons for only $1,495. After that, there's a Bronze Program available, and a Silver, and...

The Introductory Package consisted of four one-hour group lessons to be completed within a ten-day period. We met other couples who were starting that same evening, and were impressed with how motivated they seemed. Introducing ourselves, we learned everyone but us was training to look good at a wedding reception, an anniversary party, or some other important occasion. They were serious. They were there to learn. Dancing was no laughing matter to them, and they were determined to get their money's worth.

We had no such incentive. We were there because our good friend Anne had given us the Arthur Murray Introductory Package. We were there to have fun.

The Arthur Murray people were very nice—serious, but nice. They're accustomed to students being serious about improving their dancing. We didn't have anything to improve. For years all we'd ever done is walk in tight circles clockwise in slow dances, or jump around and flail to the beat of more vigorous rock 'n' roll. As dancers, we were starting below zero.

Arthur Murray himself began giving dance lessons in 1912 at age seventeen. He opened the first franchised Arthur Murray Studio in 1925; today there are 270. Arthur married his dance partner, Kathryn, in 1925, and lived a long life—a tribute to healthy dancing, no doubt. He retired in 1964 and died in 1991. Many earnest dance instructors have carried on his legacy; they've helped thousands reach their dancing goals. But we didn't have any.

Pamela and I were one of six fidgety couples milling about on an expanse of scuffed wooden floor. It looked and smelled like old gym maple without the painted lines. We waited for Wayne to welcome us. We knew his name and his manager role from his unctuous self-introduction when we first stumbled in out of the rain, a long half-hour before.

When the formal welcome was over, Wayne was replaced by three instructors, a pair of whom demonstrated the "closed position." As near as I can tell, the closed position is the dancer's equivalent of the "ready, set" that precedes a runner's "go." We clasped each other as directed: Pamela's right hand in my left, our other arms extended at shoulder level as if holding each other at bay, shoulders back, chins up, frames upright.

With a winning smile, Wanda introduced herself, then circled us, prodding our elbows, shoulders, and chins until we stiffly approximated the prescribed position. In a cheery voice she launched into a patter so practiced it sounded pre-recorded.

Two instructors had demonstrated the box step, a basic dance movement ingeniously named after the pattern it creates on the floor. It's a standard step in ballroom dance, basic to both waltz and foxtrot. It's rudimentary. I hear even young children can perform flawless box steps after just fifteen minutes.

Wanda instructed, "John, step forward with your left foot, and Pamela, you do the mirror opposite. Okay, John: Forward-side-together; backwards-side-together. Good!"

Pamela winced.

"Getting your toes stepped on is just part of learning," Wanda's recording continued, smile unabated.

"See how easy it is? In other dances you'll be learning, the box may start from the left or right foot, either back or forward, or even sidewise. When you do the Samba de Gafieira, the leader in the Quadrado figure goes left-together-back, right-together-forward."

Wanda didn't notice she'd stunned us motionless. Music had started.

"In the waltz, the rhythm is '*One*-two-three, *four*-five-six.' Hear it?"

We nodded dutifully but had no idea what she meant. We'd known going in we were dance-impaired, but right then we saw how truly hopeless we were. All four of our left feet may as well have been in irons.

Wanda must have seen the "Huh?" on my face. She came and put her hand on my shoulder, and when her recitation of "*Four*-five-six" came back around to "*One*," she pressed her knee into the back of mine and made me step forward in time.

"There. Feel it?"

Of course I'd felt her knee, but I wasn't sure about the music.

If we made all our steps equal in length we would end up where we started each time we completed a box, so Wanda had us extend the first step a little so we would advance, I forward and Pamela backward, across the dance floor. We stopped giggling long enough to do it correctly three consecutive times.

"Hey, not bad!" I said, and immediately tripped. Stubbed toes notwithstanding, we exploded into laughter again. You know how hard it is to not laugh when you're not supposed to.

Okay. Get a grip. Closed position. Listen. *One*-two-three, *four*-five-six, start! Pamela stepped back just as I stepped forward, and we were off! Here we go! I closed my eyes to concentrate on the steps and the rhythm. I don't know how many consecutive box steps we successfully performed. Wanda even left us to assist other students, and for a few moments we were actually dancing. We're getting it! This is great! *One*-two-three, *four*-five-six; *one*-two-three, *four*-five-six…

More or less in time with the music, we shuffled, eyes closed, locked in the open position, concentrating, starting to feel hopeful, then really good about ourselves, as we box-stepped all the way across the floor. That is, until our progress was abruptly terminated when we danced straight into a wall! What had been barely contained mirth exploded again into hilarity. We laughed so hard we slid down the wall and sat heavily on the well-worn wood, out of breath.

We lost it. Just looking at each other sent us over the edge. I think Wanda worried she'd lost *us*. She clopped over in her dancing heels and towed us back to the middle of the floor to start again.

"You sure are having a good time!" she smiled.

We were.

Pamela and I were dismal as students, but that didn't prevent our Introductory Package from being uproarious fun as well as an uplifting, freeing experience in an unexpected way. You see, Pamela had taken dance lessons as a girl in Iowa, and she had memories.

The internationally renowned Dieman-Bennett Dance Theatre of the Hemispheres began in the early 1950s when

Edna Dieman and Julia Bennett began teaching dance in the Cedar Rapids YWCA. A few years later, Pamela's mom took her young daughter to Dieman-Bennett for beginner's ballet lessons, taught personally by the strict and formidable Miss Dieman. (Yes, it's pronounced *demon.*) There we were at Arthur's, decades later, when Pamela realized she still had a deeply ingrained dance-floor fear of *doing it wrong*. Our comedy of missteps exhumed the painful memory, and hitting the wall must have popped it right out of her. Seated on Arthur's floor, she finally faced the Dieman.

Our stomachs ached from laughing ourselves silly after the wall encounter. We enjoyed the remaining three lessons in our Introductory Package. We still giggle about it. We never got past the box step, though we stumbled through the final two hours trying to add turns to it.

At the end, Wanda escorted us to a small office for the "only-fourteen-ninety-five-Foundation-Program" pitch. A couple in their thirties emerged from the small room as we were ushered toward it. They wore the tight smiles you see on car buyers at dealerships. They'd gone for the Foundation Program. Their wedding—her second, his third—was just six weeks away, and they were determined to be the dancing stars of their own show.

We sat as directed in the small office. For the first time since Lesson One we were showered with Wayne's saccharine sincerity, but it didn't last long. He saw right away we were not Foundation Program material. Maybe our laughter gave us away.

A few months later, at the wedding reception for a friend's daughter, Pamela and I walked in tight circles to the slow songs and jumped and flailed to the fast ones. We had a great time. Arthur had already become just a legend.

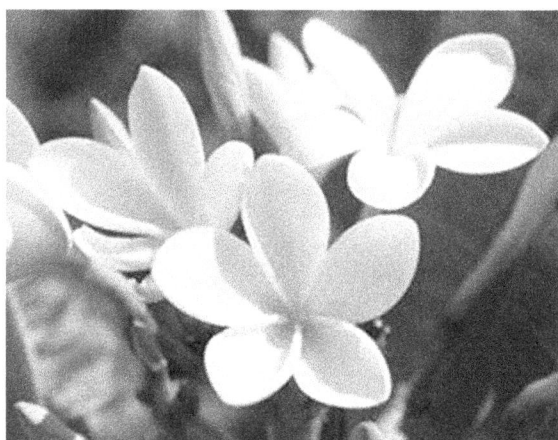

American Distress

Buying a vacation resort timeshare was the second dumbest financial decision I ever made. Buying a *second* timeshare was the first.

They're expensive to purchase and use, and, let's face it, close to impossible to re-sell. Lord, we've tried! It even costs to give them away. The annual maintenance fees rise year by year, protected by titanium-clad contracts you can't walk away from without a nasty credit hit.

Of course this enlightenment came too late.

What Pamela and I later came to call our "timeshare blues" didn't start that way. It began on a family-and-friends trip to Maui—a whole week's party to celebrate our daughter's and her husband's first anniversary. They hadn't wanted a big wedding a year before, so this was the big bash that hadn't been.

Towards the end of the Maui week, Pamela and I wandered into a handsome beachfront hotel adjacent to where we were staying on the Kaanapali coast, and right into a timeshare pitch.

Now, I ran a multimillion-dollar company for thirty years, held my own with bankers, the IRS, CPAs, corporate directors, and shareholders. I've navigated minefields set by car salesmen, insurance pitchmen, real estate agents, and stockbrokers, and emerged, if not undamaged, with dignity intact.

Maybe it was the plumeria-scented, skin-caressing tropical breeze, or the brilliant sky and sea framing the view of Lanai from the beach. Blame the cup of fragrant, steaming Kona coffee placed in my hand, or the fabulous, relaxing week we'd just spent falling in love with Hawaii yet again. Whatever it was, my guard was down, I wasn't at the top of my game, and when the young salesman trolled the timeshare lure past, I took it. I bit hard. Two weeks' worth. I felt him set the hook, and didn't even fight. Involuntarily, my American Express card was in my hand. In retrospect, I should have left home without it.

That wasn't so many years ago, but times were different. We were in an affluent bubble period of our lives, an era preceded by decades of abundant happiness but less money, and followed since by also-happy years of relative financial modesty. But at the time, there on Maui, we felt rich in every way. Effortlessly, my suntan-oiled mind generated a succession of slick rationalizations: *The kids will love it. We'll take more vacations together. Two bedrooms? Two weeks? Upgrade to ocean view? Of course!*

Instead of putting more into our IRAs, we became timeshare owners.

One of their selling points is the ability to exchange timeshare use at "any of thousands of other fine resorts throughout the world." Pamela studied the catalog and arranged a week at a Pacific beachfront resort in Mazatlán, Mexico, about eight months later.

You know what happened next. It's embarrassing enough to admit, and to explain *how* it happened; I can't tell you *why*. Remember the old Robert Redford, Paul Newman movie, *The Sting*? The Mazatlán timeshare sales operation was so polished it made our laid-back Maui experience look amateur. An army of bilingual procurers roam tourist areas from the airport to the *Zona Dorada*, approaching and affably but firmly befriending visitors, and offering gifts just to "come see the resort, have a tour, listen to what we have to offer; it's only ninety minutes of your time, no obligation, and we give you $200." The money is cash, and it ain't pesos. *Gotcha.*

Pamela and I were lingering in a popular oceanfront establishment, La Costa Marinera, after a great lunch, when a middle-aged woman we at first mistook for a fellow tourist came by our table, introduced herself, and began innocent small talk. By the time she revealed her real motivation we were already thinking how nice a person she was and how harmless it would be to just go have a look. After all, we were on vacation and didn't have much to do but see stuff, her pictures of the resort were gorgeous, and who can't use an extra $200?

Procurers are paid per capita to deliver prospects to the resorts and hand them over to the sales team. As soon as she accomplished this task the next morning, our new BFF vanished back into the sea of Americans and Canadians arriving every day to escape the weather or whatever back home. We turned around, and she was already gone.

There, instead, was Ana, our guide for the resort tour. Her job was to impress us with the property's beauty, marvelous amenities, and the available options in timeshare units. Accommodations ranged in size from a spacious single room with bath and kitchenette to a presidential suite, and that was surpassed by a top-end, luxury three-master-bedroom villa with private pool and personal concierge service. Her questions about our family, travel preferences, hobbies, et cetera, were deftly converted to reasons why owning a time-share at the resort would be perfect for us. It was a low-pressure, rather pleasant half hour. The resort is indeed a tropical paradise and sells itself.

We were returned to the sales center and turned over to the nice but more businesslike Maria Elena, who explained in detail and excellent English how affordable ownership would be. Finally, having been softened by Ana and enlightened by Maria Elena, we were introduced to George, an aging, paunchy ex-pat American with a well-oiled used-car-dealer demeanor: the closer.

George looked like someone you wouldn't trust to help his own mother cross the street. His flushed jowls hung bulldog-like, and at regular intervals he wiped sweat from his bald pate with a limp, once-white cloth. He spoke in a soft drawl we later learned was South Carolinian, but could have been an act. Oozing sincerity, he shook my hand. His engulfed mine.

Pamela and I gave each other knowing glances. We knew the drill. We were prepared. We'd been through Maui just months before, after all, and we were wise to the tactics. We'd already been there for more than the agreed ninety minutes. All we had to do was say *no*, collect our $200, and go back to our other, admittedly lesser quality, timeshare.

But George was good. Real good.

"You folks enjoying getting to know the resort," he asked without a question mark. "Let's say we take a little break. You two go have a really nice lunch on me at our restaurant right over there, and I'll see you after. How's that sound," he said, again no question mark.

Pelicans skimmed Emerald Bay; slow-motion flamingoes strutted in a nearby pond. Below arching coconut palms, an impressive iguana sunned itself on a rock. As we dabbed our lips with linen napkins a final time, George ambled over and pulled up a chair at our umbrella-shaded glass table. As on Maui, plumerias grow well on the Mexican Riviera. Their floral fragrance is often described as "intoxicating," and it's true. There were some in bloom close to where we sat, sated.

"Food's great here, isn't it," the smiling big George stated, not queried. At least he didn't have bad teeth.

I admit we liked being spoken to as if we were people of ample monetary means. Picking up all the signals, the crafty veteran George went right for the kill: the Villa, perfect for the family stays we were already imagining. Giddy, definitely not in our right minds, plumeria essence wafting, we signed paperwork for two Villa weeks a year for twice what we'd paid on Maui, and committed ourselves to an eternity of hefty, annually rising maintenance fees.

And for years, we didn't care much. We were in that afflu-ent bubble period of our lives and made the most of both timeshares. We returned to Maui and Mazatlán again and again, went to Paris and Cabo San Lucas and several fine U.S. resorts, gave weeks as gifts to family and friends, and thor-oughly enjoyed all of it.

But things change. I'd subscribed to the myth that vaca-tions shouldn't be stressful, but the ongoing costs, once easy, became problematic, then onerous. I began the search for a way out. A couple years later, reality landed with the *plop!* of a dropping coconut. For Mazatlán, anyway, the only way out was to walk. My brother Dave, a finance executive, helped me get past my feelings. *Sunk cost* is the accounting term for unrecoverable past expenditures. Dave got through to me that no good decision is ever made looking back and bemoaning sunk costs. You have to look forward and make choices based on future obligations and their affordability. Aha! That made the walk-away decision easier. We were done.

So, this year I paid the maintenance fee to enjoy the Mazatlán Villa for a final time. We arranged a family vacation—a week with the children and grandchildren, and a second with my brother, sister, and brother-in-law. We'd all been there together before and looked forward to returning.

Of course, everything went wonderfully: all the reasons we bought the Villa timeshare in the first place played out in two January weeks of perfect summery weather. It was great kick-back family time. We caught fish (even two marlins), had hours and hours of beach and pool time, saw whales, dolphins, sea turtles, and a gazillion birds, picked shells from the beach, played for hours and hours with the grandkids, went for long walks, almost successfully avoided sunburns, and shopped for local stuff. I wrote a little. We read a lot, ate a lot, and did a fair amount of nothing, which was the idea. My American Distress card is still bleeding, and my Visa's bruises from numerous beatings are only slowly healing, but for one last sunlit time, it was all worth it. I cannot say we didn't enjoy the illusion of playing wealthy for a while, but it's over.

Pamela and I and my siblings went to La Costa Marinera for dinner on our final evening in Mazatlán. Gently breaking surf flashed white in the light of the glowing restaurant windows, and across the half mile of shimmering black, Isla de Venados stood pale gray against a moonlit sky. Our Mazatlán timeshare career had come full circle, back to where it started. We paid our bill, my Amex card cringing and whimpering all the way to the cashier.

On our way out, I noticed both Pamela and I scanning the large dining room. Maybe she was saying *adios*, but I was secretly hoping to spot the timeshare procurer lady to thank her for all the good times. Silly, I know. Years had passed, and of course she wasn't there.

But just a few tables away, another was discreetly working the room.

A Levittown Family Tale

I grew up in Levittown, part of Hempstead Township, Long Island, New York. It was the first mass-produced suburb in the United States, and its creator, William Levitt, is credited with initiating the tract housing construction techniques that led to the explosive growth of American suburbia in the post–World War II era.

My parents bought into this new American Dream and a Levitt house in 1949. They and my friends' parents, along with a few thousand other Levittown homeowners, were patchworked together by neighborhood proximity and relative economic equality. Our World War II veteran dads earned enough to afford an early Levitt house. Many Levittown couples added on to their homes as their families grew, or moved to more upscale communities when the breadwinner dad became sufficiently successful. Now and then a family fell on hard times and had to sell. As kids, we were ignorant of financial stuff—except our own dimes and quarters—but we knew families came and went.

Mr. and Mrs. Martin were the parents of my boyhood friend Ricky and all his sisters. Mr. Martin—we were taught not to refer to adults by their first names—was an executive with a Manhattan advertising agency, and one of tens of thousands of daily Long Island Railroad commuters. Having grown a sizable family, the Martins expanded their square footage to make more space for everyone, and Ricky had his own room in the remodeled upstairs. Being the only boy had its plusses.

Neighborhood moms were all different, but they were all moms, which to us made them more alike than not. Mrs. Martin always seemed to be happy. She must have had pop music or old standards playing in her head while doing housework, because every so often a line or two would come singing out of her in clear soprano. On summer evenings Levittown windows would be open, everyone hoping for a breeze to make it all the way from Zach's Bay. From our house across the street, we'd sometimes hear Mrs. Martin's voice lilting, carrying as if it came from the sky itself. The sound hung sweetly in the warm air.

The Martins were avowed Francophiles. In their living room were framed prints of Paris cityscapes, no less entrancing for being reproductions. I could stand, stare, and imagine myself walking a Maurice Utrillo street right there in the Martin house, though the original *Rue Custine de Montmartre* resides in the Hermitage in St. Petersburg. Another framed piece on those Levitt walls, a watercolor painted by a local street artist, depicted the Parisian icon Le Moulin Rouge. The Martins' living rooms walls transported me to France, free.

We were not oblivious to volatile situations confronting America and the world in those days, but in our Levittown nest we felt relatively untouched by them. The Cold War dragged on, Sputnik dented the national ego, and JFK, a new-generation politician, became president. For most Levittowners, good times rolled on, despite the scary world. As the 1950s drew to a close, Ricky's family included four sisters and a Pomeranian he'd rescued from under a snowed-in car. In 1961 his parents fulfilled a lifelong dream: that summer the two of them went to France.

They visited Ricky's paternal grandparents in Paris, where the senior Mrs. Martin worked as secretary to an American NATO diplomat. They also took in London, Copenhagen, and Lake Como. Two weeks later they flew home, flushed with excitement and bearing photos, some new art, mementos for the kids, and remembrances to be recounted in years of stories. The trip was the best thing they'd ever done together, with the exception of creating their children. It was their once-only international excursion—the trip of their lifetimes.

Not long after they got back, word got around Mrs. Martin was expecting Number Six. Having children had been the most popular Levittown pastime in the late '40s and through the '50s, but by 1961 most of the original neighbor moms, including mine, were done having children and were busy raising them.

Ricky hoped for a baby brother. We think his parents did, too. Soon after the announcement of the Martin family addition, a new object appeared in Ricky's house: a coin bank, perched atop his mom's tall bedroom dresser. The first-trimestered Mrs. Martin confided in Ricky that she and his father had started a loose-change savings plan toward his potential brother's circumcision cost.

I couldn't believe it when Ricky told me this family secret! At fourteen, it struck us as colossally funny. Ricky swears it was my idea, and maybe it was, but we dubbed the coin receptacle the Hidden Head Bank. Formed of rubber ducky material, the bank was an eight-inch-tall bovine caricature—obviously a cow, not a bull—sitting on its haunches.

As Number Six gestated and coin deposits mounted, it became difficult for Ricky to resist making the occasional, careful withdrawal. Unfortunately, the bank's in-slot was also its only exit. Extracting coins required Ricky's adept use of a butter knife. And patience. And time. I always stood watch in the hallway. The Hidden Head Bank financed a lot of cherry Cokes at the soda fountain in Oscar's Drugstore. In an era before fetal ultrasounds, no one knew the baby wouldn't be a boy until Lisa was born in February 1962. Ricky doesn't remember what then became of the bank, but one day it was no longer there.

At that stage of our lives we weren't kids anymore, but Ricky and I and our friends weren't anything else yet, either. We felt stranded in that teenage wasteland The Who wouldn't sing about for another decade. We were too old to catch lightning bugs, too young to drive; old enough to be interested in girls but too young to do much about it. Outside of school, which we took seriously because of the Russians, sometimes we were just bored.

A favorite boredom-induced, cherry-Coke-inspired outing was to Oscar's, on the corner of Bellmore Road and Falcon Street in East Meadow, just west of Levittown—a hike from our homes. To get there we had to run across busy Wantagh Parkway. Ricky and I had known since pre-school of our IQ-minimizing effect on each other. Two otherwise smart kids could, in seconds, plummet to communal idiocy. It was quasi-suicidal to sprint across that four-lane, high-speed parkway even once, *ever*, and we did it dozens of times. Once I felt the hot breath of a passing car on my back as I leapt the last few feet to the grassy shoulder, and safety.

Not long after the youngest family member's birth, Mr. Martin lost his family-supporting job in the City. Months stretched into years of odd jobs and low-wage positions. It takes it out of a man to suffer a loss he cannot recover. Like the paper airplanes Ricky and I once coasted off the eighty-sixth floor of the Empire State Building, Mr. Martin spiraled slowly down in a looping, erratic path. In those days, mental maladies weren't talked about. None of the Martins explained why he was seldom around.

Several years later, Ricky's mom's illness was discovered. Even during treatments, Mrs. Martin kept the family together, until she just couldn't anymore. She took a job in retail and received some public assistance. Slowly, the Francophile lovers played out tales of different cancers: hers intestinal, his of the soul, both ultimately fatal.

When the Levittown Historical Society invited me to read selections from my first book, *Gift of Seeds*, in 2013, Ricky spent eight hours on a train to get to Levittown to attend. The following day, the two of us walked all over our old neighborhood. I was amazed how many names and details Ricky recalled.

"Remember the Dillmans? They lived there, and the Fullers next door. That's the Ormond house, and the Filardis lived either there or there," Ricky said, pointing. "And you remember Rona's house, of course, and the Smileys..."

Under the streetlamp at the corner of Gun and Chimney, we stopped, staring at our respective childhood homes. For a few minutes we were each too full to talk. The gap between *then* and *now* momentarily dissolved. I felt *was* and *is* conjoined, as if time didn't matter.

It was a surreal intermission. When we resumed walking, we straddled the perspectives of fourteen-year-olds and the reality of being more than half a century older.

We passed McLaren Field, and cut across to Center Lane to walk around the Village Green—scene of so many candy store treats and a few boyhood traumas at the hands of bullies. We looked into the much-changed sump, now sporting a grassy soccer field where only marsh weeds used to grow. We crossed the Wisdom Lane school grounds, recounting boyhood confessions I'll never write.

Plenty of other tales came back on that more-than-fifty-years-later walk. *She was class valedictorian, remember?... I heard he went to Canada to dodge the draft... Did his mom really run off with the Meenan Oil deliveryman?... Elaine won a full Ivy League scholarship; she became a fine teacher, like her mother... Bob didn't come back from Vietnam... I heard Angelina had three kids before she was twenty... Can you believe Freddie later became a judge?... Remember that guy from Little League? Played college ball; I hear he almost made it with the Mets...* Dozens of recollections later, a theory formed. It's an empirical approximation not factually founded, but it worked for us: Over decades, about a quarter of early Levittown families had bad stuff happen, another quarter had some really good stuff happen, and the rest had just regular stuff happen. For people we knew and knew of, this seemed to be so. The Martin family story was one of many.

The old neighborhood is smaller, the trees bigger, most houses remodeled, and the land flatter than I remembered.

But it's Levittown. And Jones Beach, once *far* away, is just a twelve-minute drive on Wantagh Parkway.

There are few original Levittowners left. New generations live in William Levitt's sturdy homes, but foolish kids probably still dash across Wantagh Parkway. Sometimes on summer evenings, cooling breezes make it all the way from Zach's Bay.

There's probably a mom, too, singing as if no one is listening.

ALL-AROUND COWBOY

A Short Story

Waking starts small. The familiar twinge of knotted neck muscles comes alive first, and then that sore tightness across his shoulder blades and drifting down his back. His mind flickers like an old black-and-white film starting up. *Three… two…one…*

Pete awakes with a start. *What time is it?* For a moment he doesn't even know what day it is.

It *is* day, though. He can tell by the light spilling through a slit between the bedroom curtains. Dust motes dance in that narrow streak of hot Amarillo sun.

Pete blinks, still fuzzy. The darkened room comes into focus as he rouses himself from his afternoon nap. He works his legs over the side of the bed and sits there for a few breaths, then draws his still-lanky six-foot-three frame up, using the mattress edge to leverage himself erect. He stretches, trying to shake the tension that stiffens his whole body into brittleness lately.

Walking with care into the living room Pete sees his new flat-screen TV, already on. He's become very fond of that big screen—big enough for even an eighty-year-old to see.

Eighty… Damn! Never thought I'd live this long.

A few more steps and he sits, heavily, in his only really comfortable chair. Pete's right hand pulls the smooth wooden lever to raise the worn footrest of the once-navy La-Z-Boy, its fabric now as faded and soft as an old pair of Wranglers. Exhaling deeply, head back on the headrest, he punches up the volume on the remote with a knobby-jointed finger.

Playing on CBS now is the rodeo Pete wanted to watch. Trevor Brazile is calf roping. He's on his way to winning another All-Around Cowboy gold buckle at the Wrangler Champions Challenge in Rapid City, South Dakota.

Damn, he's good. But what the hell kinda name for a cowboy is "Trevor"?

Pete's dad's cowboy idol was Yakima Canutt, world champion bronc rider out of the Snake River Hills area in Washington and a Hollywood stuntman and actor from the 1920s on, after his competitive rodeo career was through. Both on the circuit and later on film, Yak performed a trick called the Crupper Mount—a leap-frog over the horse's rump into the saddle. Pete's father taught Pete the stunt, and at fourteen he would show off to anybody who'd watch. He rode in his first rodeo in 1949, and that was that: Pete became a professional cowboy, a Rodeo Cowboys of America member. For him, like his father, the world revolved around rodeo.

On the high-def TV Pete can see streaks of sweat on Cody Teal's dusty face. The cowboy is gingerly letting his weight down onto a monstrous 1,800-pound bull named Eldorado. He wraps and re-wraps the rope around his gloved left hand and exhales, ready for the chute to fly open.

Somebody once called bull riding *the longest eight seconds in sports.* The phrase stuck in rodeo circles, and for good reason. Every instinct and every massive muscle in that bull wants Cody off him, and when the gate opens, Eldorado shoots out, bucking and twisting violently, stopping short and throwing his head down—everything he can to shake that cowboy off. Teal keeps his seat and is awarded eighty-eight points, enough to win the event today. He slides off the bull's back after the timer's horn sounds, but Eldorado isn't finished. He hooks his head and goes after Cody, trying to gore him with his horns. Only after the cowboy has scrambled safely over the barricade does the TV commentator say, "Whew. Way too close! Cody had to run for his life there. Proof again that bull riders who make it in rodeo never turn their backs on the animal. You never know."

Ain't that the truth.

The money is good nowadays, not like in Pete's time when only a few top cowboys could get by just rodeoing. Everybody else had to have side jobs to feed their horses and put gas in their trucks. That was a long time ago... Crap, Pete's been getting Social Security since 1999. His last professional go-around was in Calgary at the '73 Stampede. He didn't know it was going to be his last rodeo. He finished out of the money and left feeling dusty inside and out, bone-weary, and sore.

But he met Juanita while limping out of the arena. Her megawatt smile could melt a rock, but it was her gold-flecked green eyes that held him. She was too Irish looking to have a name like Juanita, and confessed she'd just taken the name because she liked the sound of it. She knew who Pete was, and they got on right away like old friends, and then more.

Pete, blue-eyed leading man looks and all, was roped and tied, and he loved it. And her.

Juanita had been a barrel racer; she knew her way around a corral. They had each been around the block more than a few times by then, and despite having lived all their lives with the smell of it, neither Juanita nor Pete would tolerate any bullshit. They fit together like a braided bull rope wrapping a rider's leather-gloved hand, and knew they'd be riding together the rest of the way, no discussion necessary. Since then, they've been breeding and raising cattle ponies on J-P Ranch, their spread outside Amarillo. It's been their shared life for forty years.

Just about every cowboy Pete ever roped or rode with is gone now. He knows that without Juanita he'd probably have died twenty years ago himself. *She's still the best thing that ever happened to me.*

The great Jim Shoulders was Pete's last contemporary, and a good friend. Jim is still considered the Babe Ruth of rodeo, and in his prime there was hardly a man who could beat him. Only the best bulls and broncs could do that. The sole cowboy to regularly challenge Jim was the younger Casey Tibbs, champion bronc rider who took three national All-Around titles during the years Shoulders was winning five.

Pete considered Jim the toughest man to ever wear a cowboy hat. How much more would he have won if he hadn't spent so much time healing up? Shoulders must have broken half the bones in his body a couple times each in his career. He once switched to his off hand to bull ride when his better hand was busted up. He won, too.

Pete had his share of broken bones and concussions. Remembering when his bulldogging pony rolled over on him still makes him wince; even after two operations the knee has never been the same. He had his jaw reconstructed after a big Brahma stomped on his face in Cheyenne. And concussions? In the '50s the treatment for getting knocked unconscious was to throw water on the guy lying in the dust, then help him up to get ready for his next go-around.

What days those were! Sometimes they'd drive all night in an old pickup and arrive at the arena dog-tired. But when people filled the stands and the PA announcer welcomed everybody, men and beasts alike felt the energy, the excitement, and nobody worried about danger.

And the women. *Oh, man!* There was a time when all Pete had to do was touch the brim of his Resistol, nod, and smile. That was before Juanita, of course.

Pete watches the televised rodeo between his feet. When he's lying back and comfortable he's not mindful of old aches. He won't take prescription pills, preferring to nurse a little Jack now and then. Works better on the mind.

On the screen, Trevor Knowles—*another Trevor!*—is readying for his final steer wrestling go-around. Two gated rider's boxes and the chute between them are filled: Knowles on his horse in the left box, a 580-pound steer squeezed in the narrow chute, and in the right box, the hazer—another cowboy to ride alongside the steer to keep it from veering off.

The chute gate springs open and the steer dashes out into the arena dust. Two blinks later a string trailing the full-speed steer pulls taught, instantly releasing the cowboys' gates. Bulldogger's and hazer's mounts reach full gallop two strides into the arena, gaining on the steer, and Knowles is already leaning way over to drop out of his saddle onto the steer, plow his boot heels into the dirt, and throw the animal by its horn and nose. The whole thing takes 5.7 seconds. Best time of the day. A work of kinetic western art.

Pete knows steer wrestling *feels* a lot longer than those few seconds. Watching the bulldogger on the big screen, he can still feel a horse's muscles ripple under him, and the strong scents of animals, worn leather, dust, sweat, and fear mingle in his nostrils. He closes his eyes and sees a young Pete's hands on the reins.

The memory plays out like a grainy 8mm film, not the sharp, brilliant colors of digital HD. Pete knows it's not real, but for just a few seconds there he feels like an all-around cowboy again.

*The ultimate measure of a man
is not where he stands in moments of comfort
and convenience,
but where he stands at times of challenge and controversy.*

—Martin Luther King

The Fresh Air Kid

By 1960, Dr. Martin Luther King's moral leadership had lifted him to international prominence. That spring and summer, in cities and towns across the South, civil rights proponents staged sit-ins at lunch counters to protest racial discrimination. For the fifteen years since World War II, perseverance had put pressure on the old ways. Step after step—some halting, some graceful, a few historic, most too small to be remembered—change kept coming. Massive icefields of prejudice had started to show cracks.

There were no black families in Levittown, New York, for the first decade and more of its existence. All the kids in school—as well as the teachers and all the parents—wore skins in various hues of alabaster, from pale pinkish to freckled to the faintest of olive, all reflecting European ancestries. No brown. No black. No yellow. White.

I knew a little about black people from childhood times spent on my grandmother's farm in Delaware. I knew Brad, my uncle's primary farmhand. I knew he was kind. But few friends and classmates in our hometown had exposure to anybody not like us.

My boyhood friend Ricky and I were of the local majority. Ricky lived on Chimney Lane in one of the ten houses whose backyards bordered the McLaren Field grounds. Beyond his low fence, it was as if Ricky's yard extended like a vast sea of weedy grass stretching south all the way to the playground near Cliff Lane.

Since 1877, The Fresh Air Fund has been helping thousands of inner-city New York children spend a week or two with volunteer families in the suburbs and countryside. The Levittown Presbyterian Church was a sponsor, and Ricky's parents, active church members, qualified to host a Fresh Air Fund kid.

They met Bernie when his bus arrived in the church parking lot on a warm July afternoon in 1960. Like the rest of the nervous black kids on the Fresh Air Fund charter, Bernie was from the middle of high-density Brooklyn. He was twelve but looked older to me. This was to be his first time out of the city for longer than a day.

We three were about the same age, but some of the stuff Ricky and I took for granted was probably new to Bernie. To him, ours was certainly the suburb of Wally and Beaver Cleaver: lawns and sprinklers to run through, trees to climb, the vast ball field just over the fence from Ricky's backyard, bikes to ride, the woods along Wantagh Parkway... The first week of Bernie's stay flew by, each day filled doing the things we usually did—*except* for going to the Bluegrass Lane swimming pool, or Jones Beach, or even the Center Lane Village Green candy store. Ricky's mom deftly steered play choices in other directions without saying why.

Our natural science explorations included catching toads, lightning bugs, garter snakes, and butterflies. I don't really know if these were firsts to Bernie, but Ricky and I were eager to show off our suburban world, and he enjoyed it all. For Bernie, his two weeks in Levittown were a vacation.

At that age Ricky and I couldn't yet see how insular our world was; our small town was all we knew. Bernie had an aura of a bigger "elsewhere" about him that we couldn't comprehend. He carried himself with polite assurance and a kind of poise we could admire but wouldn't understand for years. We, Ricky's parents, the Levittown Presbyterian Church, and The Fresh Air Fund itself all lived the belief that we were giving every Bernie a great gift to get them out of their Brooklyn "asphalt jungle." Maybe so, but the most enduring memory of Bernie's sojourn in Levittown is his gift of "fresh air" to us.

Although Ricky's family didn't hide their guest, we didn't realize how widely word of Bernie's presence had spread. One evening in his second week, Bernie, Ricky and I were sitting on the grass on the McLaren Field grounds, just over the split-rail fence from Ricky's backyard. A night game was under way, and the field's floodlights illuminated all the way to Ricky's house. We were just hanging around, plucking tufts of grass and throwing them at each other—you know, important boy stuff. We were joking and talking idly, not about anything. The warm earth we sat on felt good.

Eight boys abruptly appeared. We hadn't noticed their approach. They came at us over the low fence, having cut through Ricky's backyard from Chimney Lane, the street in front of his house. They'd seen us sitting out back. They were looking for Bernie.

Everyone was in half-shadow from the ballpark lights. We couldn't see all their faces clearly, but we knew the boys from school. Ricky's private name for them was the "Irish Catholic Mafia."

With his gang around him, the front man, Kevin, began gesturing angrily and calling Bernie out. Kevin and several others taunted Bernie, obviously trying to goad him into a confrontation so they could beat him up and scare him back to Brooklyn.

Ricky and I felt our stomachs quiver. Our own little-kid memories of terror at the hands of Village Green bullies swept over us. This already looked really bad. We gulped air, futilely trying to settle ourselves.

Bernie got easily to his feet, facing Kevin.

"Go home, nigger! We don't want your kind in our town," Kevin hissed, jaw clenched.

"Bernie!" Ricky implored.

He moved as if to hold Bernie back. Bernie waved him off.

Kevin stood in front of his mob, fists up in a boxer's stance. His eyes glared and his face burned red in the shadowy light. Thinking back on the scene, I wonder how one almost-seventh-grader could hold such intense, irrational hatred. Kevin must have been funneling the prejudices of generations.

Bernie faced him, eight feet away, calm, hands relaxed at his sides. In a voice tight with loathing, Kevin spat more venomous words.

The Fresh Air kid just watched him.

In my gut I felt the force of the rage in Kevin's verbal firebombs. It was a scene like we'd seen only in black and white on television: a racial confrontation about to flare into violence. But this was live, real, and in color. It wasn't narrated by Walter Cronkite, and it wasn't happening hundreds of miles away in a Southern state. Right there in white-bread Levittown, spewed racial epithets marinated in raw acrimony. The menacing group had the feel of a lynch mob.

I shuddered. Right then, Ricky and I believed Bernie was about to die. Maybe we were, too.

Kevin and his cohorts kept taunting, daring Bernie to fight. Bernie just stood, unmoving.

Then Bernie laughed. Loudly. Right in their faces!

A hush held the tableau.

"You don't want to fight with me," he said in calm, measured words that carried no challenge.

For the next three silent seconds, while the Earth rotated a mile east on its axis, where we stood, nothing moved. But everything changed. Maybe it was Bernie's matter-of-fact statement, or his assurance—I don't know—but the explosion we felt was sure to happen didn't. Impossibly, Kevin lowered his hands and relaxed his fists. His shoulders sank as tension dissolved a little. We still don't know how it happened, but the fury was passing.

"C'mon, let's go," mumbled Kevin to his guys, and turned.

We watched, astounded. The rest of the Irish Catholic Mafia pivoted and walked slowly away toward the lights, Kevin last. None looked back.

We vaulted the low fence into Ricky's yard and headed for the back door. Ricky was ecstatic with incredulous relief. Bernie had stood up to Kevin and the Mafia, and they'd backed down! We didn't have words to explain what had happened, but we knew we'd witnessed courage. The term *conflict resolution* wasn't in our vocabularies then.

"Bernie, that was *crazy!*" Ricky said, his admiration apparent. "How'd you *do* it?"

"They're country boys," Bernie said, his smile forming. "I'm a city guy. They wouldn't stand a chance."

The way he said it, it clearly wasn't a boast. Ricky's and my insides were still buzzing with the miracle we'd witnessed, but Bernie had already left it behind.

"Hey, we gonna watch Ed Sullivan?" he reminded us. Later we joked about how the murder of a Fresh Air Fund kid wouldn't have been good for Ricky's parents or the Levittown Presbyterian Church, not to mention Bernie's mom and sister back in Brooklyn.

Dr. King never knew it, but on a hot summer night in 1960, the civil rights movement came to Levittown—a microcosm of it, anyway, in one Fresh Air kid.

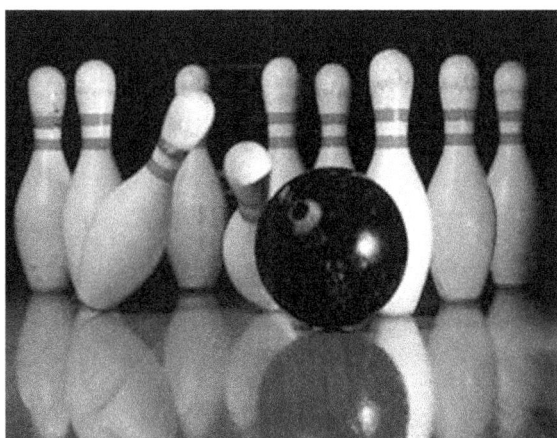

BOWLING WITH DAD

My brother Dave and I were in our father's room at Village Healthcare for the last time the three of us would be together. January 2011 had a little more than a week left in it, and Dad, age ninety-three, would slip away on February 6. Other family members visited him that shining Saturday, but for part of the afternoon it was just Dad, Dave, and me.

A bowling show was on the television. Dad was awake but drifting, as he did more and more in those ebbing days. Maybe there wasn't much more to talk about right then, anyway. Our ears perked to the characteristic crash of ten pins exploding in a perfect strike, and attentions turned like compass needles to the TV.

The bowling program was the *2011 Tournament of Champions*, returned to ABC for the first time in over thirteen years. Nelson Burton Jr.'s still-familiar voice was delivering memory-lane references to the venerable *Pro Bowlers Tour* on ABC, once a bowling fan's mainstay. In the second game of the live telecast, Mika Koivuniemi held viewers like us rapt, rolling eleven straight strikes before leaving a tenpin and falling just short of a perfect game. Mika's opponent fared far worse, leaving splits and missing spares and ending up with the incredible score of 100, the lowest point total in the history of the Professional Bowlers Tour.

Dad, Dave, and I watched this historic event in a bubble that encapsulated us and the TV and excluded all extraneous. My brother and I later recounted how out-of-time it felt, and so familiar. As boys, we'd watched TV bowling with Dad many times.

Dad wasn't just a fan; he was a bowler. Competing manufacturers AMF and Brunswick brought automated pinsetters into widespread use after World War II, and from the 1950s on, bowling's popularity took off all over America. Dave's and my hometown grew rapidly, and Levittown, Long Island, sprouted its bowling alleys, too. The nearest to our house was Levittown Lanes at the North Village Green, and Dad bowled in leagues there for as long as I can remember. A powerful man, he used to throw a fast, straight ball that hooked at the last moment into the one-three pocket, when it was working well. He was a decent league bowler and steady teammate, averaging in the 180s and occasionally rolling scores in the mid-200s and higher. Never a perfect game, however. He said nine strikes in a row was the best he ever did.

Once in a while he'd take me practice bowling with him. He gave me pointers but encouraged me to do what was natural for me rather than try to bowl like him. I couldn't do that anyway. This was before I had my own equipment. I rented red-white-and-blue shoes with white powder inside, and used a house ball more dented and pockmarked than a prizefighter. Dad was working on perfecting his three-stride approach. When it was my turn, I tried to keep my ball out of the gutter.

Only a few times did he take me with him on his league nights. His TWA Fliers team shirt was white with red lettering and piping, and his teammates called each other by their last names: *Tyler. L'Episcipo. Walden. Schenker. Gray.* When I was around, if a guy made a bad shot or missed an easy spare, the others would try to *shush* him before he cursed out loud. I already knew all those words anyway. I'd learned them from Dad when he worked on the car and didn't know I was listening.

Levittown Lanes had thirty-six alleys, and on league nights the place was loud, boisterous, and smelled like an ashtray. A pall of tobacco smoke hung throughout the building at head height. By the end of a three-game series the air was so thick even nonsmokers had inhaled half a pack. Tyler, a tall southpaw, threw a big, sweeping curve and bowled with a bratwurst-sized cigar clenched in his teeth. His own rank, blue-black smog made him squint at the pins, and he ate as much as smoked the stogie.

Uniformed waitresses with rhinestone glasses laughed with the bowlers, took bar orders, and delivered round trays laden with beverages. Mine was the only Coke. At any time a player could declare a "beer frame," and a teammate who didn't *mark*—throw a strike or spare—in that frame had to buy the rest a beer. The bar did a thriving business on league nights.

In the late 1950s and into the '60s, bowling shows proliferated on American television. Old *TV Guides* reveal as many as ten programs a week in some cities. The Professional Bowlers Association was formed in 1958. We used to watch *Jackpot Bowling*, the first weekly show on TV, as well as *Championship Bowling* and *Make That Spare*. In 1962 ABC began broadcasting *Professional Bowlers Tour*. Around our house, pro bowlers' names were as well known as those of New York baseball stars like Willie Mays and Mickey Mantle. Don Carter, Earl Anthony, Billy Welu, and Dick Weber; Carmen

Salvino, Ray Bluth, Steve Nagy, and more, all threw strikes in our Levittown living room. If it was Saturday afternoon, Dad would sip a Miller High Life and we'd all snack on peanuts or pretzels. Nobody'd miss a frame of the action. I can hear *Bowling Stars* announcer "Whispering" Joe Wilson describing everything *sotto voce,* as if we were his only audience.

Dad would prepare for a TV match by drawing carefully ruled score sheets on paper, then sit back in his overstuffed chair, feet on the hassock, score sheets supported by a *True* magazine in his lap, a TWA number two pencil at hand. Between sips, as the games progressed frame by frame, he'd fill the little boxes with neatly written numbers and symbols just like the scorekeeper on the black-and-white RCA.

And fifty-something years later, there we were: Dad and Dave and me, watching bowling on television again, though this time in high-definition color. I don't remember if we even saw the rest of the match after Koivuniemi got that ten-pin tap and finished with a 299. A fallen pin had rolled over and bumped the ten, but only hard enough to make it quiver, not topple.

Not a perfect ending, but almost as good as it gets.

American Motorcycle Association, Inc.

Motorcycle Speed Record

Movin' Mike

My Pamela is often the first afflicted with early drafts of my essays and stories. She's a fan, of course, and only gently critical. She receives my newborn writings eagerly, with the skill, care, and love of a veteran delivery room RN.

This one is about her dad. Pamela knew I'd been working on it. I knew it was important to her and hoped I'd done justice to the first man in her life, whom she adored.

Pamela arranged herself on the family room love seat and looked at me with soft expectancy. I held the printed pages and began to read aloud:

Mike McCann and motorsports grew up together. The first Indianapolis 500 was held May 30, 1911. Mike was born in September that year.

From adolescence on, Mike went every year from his native eastern Iowa to Indianapolis for the 500, the premier auto event of its kind. In his later years he never missed watching the race on TV. But the Indy wasn't all Mike loved. He had motor oil in his blood. He raced midgets and stock cars; competed in road rallies; ran powerboats; bought, fixed, drove, and sold scores of cars; and he revered motorcycles. If it had an internal combustion engine and was made to move on earth or water, Mike loved it. And the faster the better.

He always laughed his big laugh retelling the story of how, at age eleven, he became the family driver. The McCann family car was a two-door Ford Model T coupe with a top speed of 45 miles per hour. Mike's dad was a conservative driver, seldom going over 25. The seventeen-mile trip from their farm to the closest city, Cedar Rapids, Iowa, could take most of an hour—*forever* to Mike—so he secretly rigged a stiff cable to the engine's throttle and ran it under the Model T's floorboards to the back seat. When his dad wasn't driving fast enough for Mike's liking, Mike could pull on the cable and "give it the gas," as he put it, without his father knowing. Of course, the senior McCann caught on to Mike's trick soon enough and angrily told his son, "Okay, smart young man, from now on *you're* the family chauffeur!"

No matter how many times Mike told this story over the years, he'd always smile and laugh all the way through it, eyes sparkling. "I got what I wanted—some speed out of that old Model T—and a lot more. I got to *drive!*"

Mike's mother and father died three years apart, when Mike was fourteen and seventeen. In a scrapbook he left to his daughter was an obituary written in Mike's careful hand, words he'd penned after his father passed in the winter of 1928. Mike was a junior in high school.

"We lived in the beautiful house my parents built and equipped on our farm on the east edge of Lisbon. There my mother died on January 12, 1925, and my father on February 23, 1928, which leaves me, their only child, saddened, but with fond memories of my parents, and strength enough to send me nicely into life."

Sounds pretty formal for a seventeen-year-old, but that's what he wrote.

His aunt Clara, Mike's mother's spinster sister, took him in. The sale of his parents' property in Lisbon, Iowa—that special house and small farm—helped finance his college education. At Iowa State College in Ames, Mike studied mechanical engineering, completing his degree in 1934.

Those early years of the Great Depression saw the rise in popularity of jazz, swing, and big band music. The Charleston, favorite of the Roarin' decade, gave way to newer dances like the Lindy hop and the jitterbug. Most popular, however, were variations of the ballroom classic fox-trot, whose steps could be adapted to a range of musical tempos. Mike McCann, like many college men of his day, got those fox-trot moves down perfectly. Mike could glide across a dance floor as smoothly as he drove a race car around a track.

Even for a mechanical engineer, jobs were scarce when he graduated. Young Mike's heart and competitive drive drew him into motorsport events all over the country. The scrapbook is filled with photographs and clippings from races in Iowa, Minnesota, Ontario, Kansas, Wisconsin, Florida, Illinois, and California. There's Mike, in leather helmet and goggles, riding motorcycles with names like Anzani, Henderson, Ascot, Cyclone, Indian, and Harley. His first racing bike was a 1921 FCA twin cam he rebuilt and took to 88 miles per hour in 1930, a year out of high school. Other pictures show Mike in Indy cars, midgets, an early Chevy roadster, and winning a one-man hydroplane race on an Illinois lake. An autographed black-and-white of a smiling buddy and fellow midget racer, Karl Hattel, sits alongside an L.A.

newspaper clipping headlined, "Midget Driver Dies." Hattel's skull was fractured when he crashed his car into a guardrail. He was twenty-four. The prominent placement of his photo in the scrapbook suggests his death hit Mike hard.

Risk is accepted by the motorsports fraternity. Drivers push their machines to perform better, faster, longer—always aware something can go horribly wrong in an instant. Racers don't worry much about it, though, especially the younger ones. Win or lose, nothing beats the joy of speed. His friend's sudden death didn't deter Mike from racing.

Every summer for thirty years after World War II, Mike spent weeks at the Bonneville Salt Flats in Utah, hanging out with fellow speed lovers, smoking cigars, and peering intently at carburetors and spark plug gaps through magnifiers clipped to his round-lensed glasses. In the 2006 movie *The World's Fastest Indian*, Anthony Hopkins portrays New Zealander Herbert James "Burt" Munro, who set the Class S/A 883cc "Flying One Mile" land-speed record in 1967, pushing his garage-built "Munro Special" Indian streamliner motorcycle to 178.97 miles per hour. The film came out almost twenty years after Mike McCann was gone, but he didn't need to see it. He was *there*. Mike and the real Burt Munro were friends. They'd met at Bonneville, and Mike helped Burt ready his Indian for the record run. When I first met Mike in 1971 he'd been working on a car in his shed out back and came into the house wearing a T-shirt pulled tight over his lean frame. It had a red oval "STP" logo on the chest and "Munro Special" printed on the back.

Two years after being part of the pit crew for Munro's "fastest Indian" run, Mike accomplished a similar feat. An

American Motorcycle Association certificate acknowledges that M. E. McCann set a new motorcycle speed record in Class APS-AG-500 on the 22nd of August, 1969, on the Bonneville Salt Flats. The record was 126.379 miles per hour. Mike set it on a 1957 Norton 500, a modified Manx with aerodynamic front fairing.

This is the gist of a framed certificate hanging in a gallery of family photos in our house. Next to it is an early 1940s photo of a young Mike standing proudly beside beautiful girl-next-door Dorothea. They were married in 1941. Their only child, and my future wife, Pamela, was born to them in 1947.

During the war, Mike's work as an engineer for a Defense Department contractor placed him in Cedar Rapids. Income from the job enabled him to buy back the original McCann homestead in nearby Lisbon. It was the very house his father had built before Mike himself was born—the same property they'd had to sell when his dad died in 1928. Mike was a competitor; he'd wanted it back, and he got it. Pamela grew up in the same house her father had.

Pamela and I were married and living in the Phoenix area the first time her parents visited us. Within an hour of arriving—they'd driven all the way from Iowa—Mike challenged me to arm wrestle with him.

At first I thought he was kidding, and I jokingly declined. I was in my mid-twenties and Mike was more than twice my age.

"Come on," Mike said again. "Just once. Give it a go."

I was about to laugh the challenge off a second time, when I could tell by his tone and look he wasn't kidding. He really wanted to arm wrestle.

"Come on, give an old man a chance," he said, not smiling.

So, elbows together on a countertop, right hands locked in a firm grip, I arm wrestled my father-in-law as hard as I could for the eight seconds it took him to bend my arm back and pin it.

Mike released my hand and stood up. He didn't say another word about the challenge, then or ever, but he smiled. He must have proven something important to himself. I don't know; I was just getting to know him. Later I understood how much getting older pissed him off.

I never saw Mike and Dorothea dance together. By the time Mike retired and they moved, in 1978, to our community in California to be near their grandchildren, rheumatoid arthritis had ended her dancing days. At a community party in the late 1970s Mike wowed the younger women with his "Castor Oil Glide" fox-trot, complete with feather steps, fancy turns, and smooth transitions. Think Fred Astaire's footwork, but performed like an engineer, with well-oiled, perfectly executed steps. Several of the more accomplished female dancers took turns being led effortlessly around the floor. Mike didn't have Fred's showmanship, or his tux and tails, but that guy could *move*!

Motorcycle racing is a younger man's sport. Mike was fifty-eight years old when he set that speed record, and it held up for years. But he didn't get back to Bonneville as much later in his life. When he couldn't race or compete for speed records anymore, he'd challenge himself. From our place out to the highway was a mile and a half of private road, most of it gently sloping downhill. In his seventies by then, Mike used to coast his '68 Chevy Impala down that road as far as it would go before he'd pop the clutch to start the 327 V-8. His goal was to get all the way to the main road, and he made it a few times. His smile revealed pride when he told me of the accomplishment. "Saves on gas, too," he added.

Less than two years after Dorothea passed away in 1985, Mike, a lifelong smoker, got the lung cancer news. He was seventy-five. Within weeks, the tumors proliferated. Mike coasted down the driveway. He had driven his last race, danced his last dance, and he left as fast as he'd lived.

As I read these last words I looked up to see Pamela quietly crying, awash in her memories and feelings. The relationship between her and her late father still runs deep as the rich Iowa soil and as straight as corn rows disappearing over the horizon.

...we have salt in our blood, in our sweat, in our tears. We are tied to the ocean.
And when we go back to the sea, whether it is to sail or to watch it,
we are going back from whence we came.

—John F. Kennedy

BOY AND THE SEA

It was early June 1976 when Pamela and I and our young son moved from Glendale, Arizona, to Oceanside, California. Broc had just turned seven. We settled into a suburban house, six minutes' door-to-shore drive from the Pacific Ocean. After five years in the Valley of the Sun, the transition to the gentle, more humid coastal climate was a happy one. Fog in Phoenix is as rare as a unicorn with wings. Our skins drank in the moisture.

Broc had never seen the ocean before. He'd never walked on sand, heard the surf, the gulls, smelled fish and kelp and salt air. He'd never seen freighters crawl along the horizon. The coast was all as eye-openingly new to him as Wonderland was to Alice. Iowa-raised Pamela had herself touched the Pacific but once before, and it had been years since my childhood beach days on the other coast.

Naturally, time at Oceanside beaches was a just about daily event all that summer. We watched Broc's early cautious explorations and held his hand in daring moments. As summer waxed, his trepidations gradually diminished. He'd been surprised and knocked down a few times by unexpected waves and, we were happy to see, always approached the water with a balance of respect and boldness.

Seashells aren't plentiful on that San Diego County beach. Broc's found treasures were usually rounded, colorful pebbles, and strands or even mounds of sea kelp. He liked the beached plants' rubbery feel and their sandy, salty squeakiness when he picked them up.

"What are those, Dad?" he asked me, pointing to the small, football-shaped, gas-filled bladders at the base of many of the coppery-brown, blade-shaped leaves.

I didn't know then they're called pneumatocysts, but I figured they must be for buoyancy. Though rooted and tethered to the sea floor, Pacific kelp also yearns to be close to the water's sunlit surface. The tops of kelp forests can form floating islands, providing refuge to myriad fish and sea creatures. These coastal kelp formations are vital to the ocean's ecosystem. Sometimes tides, waves, or propellers break long strands loose to wash ashore.

The beach was Broc's sandbox, and popping pneumatocysts became a favorite pastime. To pop one, all you have to do is grip the one-inch rubbery sac between thumb and forefinger, and squeeze. It's Nature's BubbleWrap.

Most, though, were too tough for Broc's small fingers to pop. "Dad, pop some more!" he'd implore. Before long, he discovered he could usually do it himself by stomping on them with his heel. Broc could spend hours running in ankle-deep foam and leaping on beached kelp, his white-blonde hair bouncing.

We don't have to understand the ocean to have a relationship with it. We humans have a primordial, mystical kinship with water. We don't have to know why the sea is salty, or how the ocean mothers the planet's immense water cycle, or all the mysteries that live in the deep. Like countless millions of human beings before us, the time comes when we first stand on one tiny stretch of shore and are personally introduced to the largest presence on the Earth's surface. Other than the sky, an ocean is the biggest thing we ever see in this life.

When I was Broc's age, it was Jones Beach on the south shore of Long Island. I don't remember the first time I saw the Atlantic; I was too little. I grew up with it. The beach was a friend, the shallows a playground. Even when I was older and a strong swimmer, however, deep water always felt somewhat foreboding. You can't see what's down there.

As things turned out, 1976 was our only summer in Oceanside. The nation celebrated its bicentennial that Fourth of July, and the fireworks exploding above the Oceanside Pier were spectacular. I was drawn to watch their reflections on the sea as much as the light show in the night sky.

It was the summer Broc made friends with the ocean.

*If you approach each new person you meet in a spirit of adventure,
you will find yourself endlessly fascinated
by the new channels of thought and experience and
personality that you encounter.*

—Eleanor Roosevelt

DMV Day

The letter from the California Department of Motor Vehicles said I couldn't renew my driver's license by mail this time. I had to go to a DMV office and do it in person.

Okay, I thought. *Fair enough. They want a new mug shot.* I favored the less-wrinkled, forty-something guy with brown hair on my existing license, but they wanted the weathered, white-haired guy. I understood.

I checked online for the nearest DMV office. The official website lists 181 offices statewide. Until yesterday I hadn't been to any in twenty years.

Those offices serve the more than twenty-five million licensed drivers in California. I did the math: If we each go to the DMV in person every two or three years for some reason—license renewals, plates, title transfers, ID cards, whatever—about three hundred people, on average, will show up at every DMV office every business day.

Yesterday, all of the Temecula DMV's daily three hundred were in line at 8:00 a.m. I parked four blocks away, then joined the tail of the line snaking around the building. I hadn't come prepared for the peril of sunburn, and by the time my place in line reached the entrance at about 9:15, the area of my scalp where I'm lacking white foliage was a glowing pink.

Inside! Relief was short-lived, though. It was cooler, but the line continued another half hour to a counter where I was handed a small square of paper with a letter and three-digit number on it. The code represented the order in which I was to be served, eventually, at one of fifteen windows. The sneaky part of the code wasn't the number—those progressed in their expected sequences—but the letters preceding the numbers. They're called at random. I held G075.

I scanned the waiting room. I knew it would be crowded, but every hard-seated chair in every row was filled. The walls were lined two- and three-deep with people standing. At irregular intervals, announcements came from the acoustic-paneled ceiling in a pleasant female computer-voice, and codes synchronously appeared on monitors. "Now serving B013 at window nine." The holder of ticket B013 stood, sighed, and made her way forward.

I took a place in a throng standing to one side of the harshly fluorescent-lit, stereotypical government office. The air conditioning was barely coping with the heat radiating from our bodies. It was not yet 10:00 a.m. My DMV adventure was already two hours along, and the latest "G" codes announced were only G009 and G010. Letters A through J kept having their turns as well, but not in any recognizable order. It was clearly going to be a lengthy wait until the G's rose all the way to 075.

When I received the DMV's letter, I thought, *I'll just go tomorrow morning and get it over with.* While scouting the office locations listing, I paid no attention to their website invitation to make an appointment in advance. Clearly a mistake. The crowd I surveyed from my vantage point were, like me, people without appointments.

And what a mélange we were! Every ethnicity, age, and gender in the state was represented.

Most nervous were parents of teens about to take their first behind-the-wheel test. One paunchy, business-suited dad couldn't sit still; he squirmed, stood, paced, sat, and squirmed some more as his teenage daughter tried to shrink and hide in her tablet. A well-heeled mom pushed her pimply son to the counter when his turn came. Hard to tell if his reddened face was due to complexion issues or chagrin. I guessed both.

An angry middle-aged Vietnamese man demonstrated his command of American slang, muttering his four-letter frustration more than loudly enough for many to hear. But most people sat quietly, heads down, hands in laps. A minister might have mistaken us for a reverent congregation, but the objects of worship were smartphones. The DMV provided Wi-Fi access.

At about 11:00 a chair became available. I offered it first to an older man, who declined with a kind gesture I took to mean, "No, after you." I nodded acceptance. I was glad to sit down. Then I realized, to him, *I* was the older man.

A through J codes were intoned from on high by the never-changing female voice. Despite her precise consistency, her tone grew increasingly eerie. The G's crept ahead to 038.

Now seated, my new point of view was toward the counter and numbered agent stations stretching the width of the room. I people-watched from this perspective, observing fellow captives' body shapes, sizes, and idiosyncrasies, rear view.

Some stood erect and still at the counter, hands at their sides as if facing the principal at school. Some organized their belongings on the countertop before engaging with the agent. Others shifted their weight rhythmically from one leg to the other. Still others leaned forward with elbows on the gray Formica counter, unwittingly mooning the audience assembled behind them. A woman of width wore tight Lycra pants with narrow black-and-white horizontal stripes. Had she consulted anyone about the pants making her butt look big, she might have worn something else.

I watched a DMV staffer show a petite, elderly woman with a walker to an open booth against a wall. The kind agent patiently instructed the woman how to indicate her answers to the driver's test glowing before her on the computer screen. I understand it's a twenty-question quiz. About half an hour later, the woman sat back and looked around until the same DMV lady returned and led her out of my view to a special window for her test results. My attention turned to others, but later I saw the woman making her way back through the room toward the entrance. She was accompanied by her son, who looked to be about my age. Their physical resemblance—distinctive noses—hinted at their relationship, but he confirmed it when he said, as they went slowly by me, "This way, Mom," and gently nudged her shoulder until she turned her walker toward the exit aisle. She was smiling.

"I passed," she said to him. "And they gave me ten years."

Maybe it's a strategy to reduce future crowding at DMV offices.

It was nearly 1:00 p.m. when computer lady announced, "Now serving G075 at window three." I'd been there almost five hours. My legs were stiff when I stood to head toward window three. I didn't need the reminder that I'm not the guy pictured on my old license anymore.

I paid the $33 renewal fee, signed a form, and was asked if anything had changed in my physical description. I pointed to my hair. I then correctly read aloud line six on the eye chart with my left eye and line four with my right. In forty-five seconds I was directed to have my photo and thumbprint taken around a corner in the far back of the room. When I arrived, there was no line! I looked around, expecting a throng I wouldn't want to cut in front of, when the same pleasant DMV lady who had assisted the woman with the walker earlier smiled right at me and said, "Next."

Press and hold right thumb on scanner, a quick flash of camera, and my day at the DMV ended abruptly. "All set, Mr. Gray. You'll receive your new license in the mail in about two weeks."

Only at the Department of Motor Vehicles, in a courthouse awaiting jury selection, or maybe at a Dodger game, do we get to see the wonderful diversity of humanity we are.

I actually enjoyed it. But next time I'll make an appointment.

THE ELEMENO EFFECT

The English alphabet is composed of twenty-six letters: A through Z, of course. Though formally introduced to the ABCs at age four or five, many children begin their pre-kindergarten year having already memorized the familiar sing-song recitation: *A, B, C, D, E, F, G, H, I, J, K, L, M, N, O, P...* Parents swell proudly when *their* Smartest Child Ever Born performs.

To adult ears it sounds like the child is reciting all twenty-six letters, but to many preschoolers the alphabet consists of only twenty-three letters, with an especially odd one about midway. It's the letter with longest name of all: *elemeno.*

Kids are guileless. New life mysteries reveal themselves every day, so nothing's strange about a letter with a name as long as *elemeno.* It's no stranger than *double-you*, which is also a pretty long name for a letter, though it looks like a double V. And until kids start to learn that letters are for spelling words, believing in elemeno presents no problem, and parents and teachers are none the wiser.

In the ensuing pre-K weeks or months before illumination, elemeno enjoys blind acceptance. Epiphany arrives as, one by one, preschoolers realize elemeno is really *four* letters stuck together. No longer conjoined, they are freed to become the first letters of important words, like *let, mop, new,* and *old.*

We know the elemeno effect is not limited to young children. Most of us were once believers ourselves. Literati use terms like *malapropisms*, *eggcorns*, *mondegreens*, and *spoonerisms* to describe these phenomena in adults, but I believe all have their roots in elemeno. Let's admit it: we've all had secret malformed words or phrases, often trapped for years in subconscious eddies.

At ballgames, my friend Carlos, now fifty-something, still absent-mindedly sings the opening phrase of the national anthem just as he remembers it from Esqueda Elementary in Santa Ana: *"José, can you see?..."* My wife confessed that until recently she thought *euthanasia* was one of Apple's primary target markets. And was duct tape really designed for repairing damaged mallards?

But children give us the most innocent examples. According to more than one first-grader's version of the Pledge of Allegiance, we live in o*ne nation under God, invisible, with liver tea and justice for all.*

Generation after generation, it starts all over again with elemeno. (Oh, and remember *gozinta?* Of course...it's the key to doing long division!)

Coming of Rain

A Short Story

In the pre-Andean foothills above Santa Isabel, midsummer's dawn banishes what little coolness it's taken all night to earn. Heat and humidity build to a smothering swamp by midday. In early afternoon even the breezes *siesta*, and a patina of sweat glistens on everything.

Most afternoons, the aging *señora* spends three or four hours in her suite in the hacienda. Her household staff, vineyard workers, gardeners, and grooms are freed to take their meals, sigh, and rest. For some, however, those are lesser reasons to anticipate the interlude. For Pablo and Carlota, it is their time.

Pablo washes himself after the morning hours spent tending malbec vines. As on almost every afternoon, he walks through the laundry and enters the linen room inside it. Sometimes Carlota is already there, but today he's arrived first. He slips off his shoes, slides them under the cot with his foot, and folds his *pantalones* on the straight-back chair. He stands at the linen room's small window, his back to the door, removing his shirt. The window frames a massive mango tree. The room glows white, redolent of clean cotton.

Hearing the door open, he turns as Carlota peeks in, enters, and locks the door behind her. She is already hastily shedding her *pechera*, the formal maid's uniform *la señora* insists she wear on duty. Pablo's breath quickens. Despite the heat, he shivers when Carlota smiles at him with her whole body. He drinks in her gold-flecked hazel gaze. Her softness melts against his chest. Their contact re-ignites the wildfire they share, and it engulfs them again.

A drumfire of thunder rumbles down from the hills above the town. Santa Isabel waits, hoping rain will come soon to bring sweet release from the imprisoning heat. January days always hold the prayer of an afternoon shower, but often the possibility dissolves as clouds rush east to dissipate over the plains, leaving behind flaccid air and but a tease of moisture. Today, though, a thunderstorm amasses above the mountains and moves downward, soothing the parched sky in its path. Locals know this one is big enough to boom and blow, burst and soak. Anticipation tingles through the village.

Carlota and Pedro listen to the storm's quickening breath, and to each other's. Their bodies engage in a practiced dance on the cot's damp sheets.

The storm sweeps over the hacienda, its winds making the house tremble. Booming thunderclaps come close together. Pablo is glad Carlota need not be quiet today. To the tempest's urgent rhythm, their taut, wet skins slide against each other.

The storm's intensity crests in a finale of electrical discharges and rippling thunder. The hacienda, and the cot, shudder. Outside, first large drops announce the downpour.

Santa Isabel sighs, and the rains come.

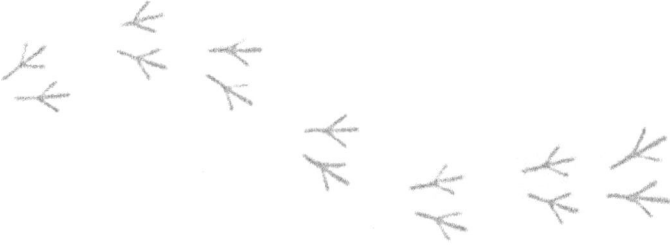

TO THE LAST BITE

I lost a lifelong friend yesterday. For over fifty years I knew him intimately, though not by name. The dentist called him Number Fifteen, one of my four twelve-year molars and a veteran of mastications too numerous to mention. It was sad to see this loyal buddy go; we shared roots, after all. For over five decades he knew everything I ever ate or drank and most of anything else I did with my mouth. We were that close.

Number Fifteen's demise wasn't unanticipated. More than twenty-five years ago a dentist, now long-retired, first told me the molar's days were numbered. "It's just a question of when," he advised. Over the years, two other dentists, six highly professional hygienists, and one expensive periodontist all pronounced similar sentences. Number Fifteen's days were indeed numbered, but it turned out to be a pretty big number.

Alas, yesterday—nearly ten thousand days and some thirty thousand meals later, not to mention innumerable snacks and sticks of gum—it came time for Number Fifteen to give up the ghost. I could have said "bite the dust," but that would be insensitive. He can't bite anything now.

Toward the end I wished Number Fifteen were less sensitive himself. You see, he'd reached the point where he couldn't take the cold anymore, and the pressure of everyday work had gradually worn his nerves raw. In his final weeks he could, without warning, emit sudden, silent, cranial-splitting screams right in the middle of otherwise enjoyable repasts. Worst of all, he was losing his grip on my left maxillary bone.

After examining x-rays, my current longtime dentist shook his head slowly and *tsk*ed a little behind his sterile mask. "It won't be long now," he said, more to the molar than to me. This doctor has presided over many dental deaths in his career, but I could feel his sadness and resignation at losing another. Or maybe he was mourning the loss of the nice little income stream he'd derived from Number Fifteen. For years that high-maintenance molar had received more attention and special treatment than all his thirty-one siblings combined.

But now he was beyond the reach of heroic measures. I reclined in the dentist's chair, growing numb, awaiting the final deed. I was grateful the pain in my head and in my wallet would both soon be over. If the tooth be known, Number Fifteen's pockets were deeper than mine.

IF I DIE THURSDAY

If, like me, you're of a certain age, you've been noticing—maybe alarmed by—unavoidable signs of your body getting older. I know my signs; you know yours. We don't have to talk about them.

But if, like me, you're of that certain age, there's something else we can't help but see. Back before I tripped over the half-century hurdle, few of my known contemporaries were dead. Since then, year by year, it's become increasingly ordinary to hear about friends and acquaintances dying. This will happen more frequently until it's my turn.

There's nothing like pondering mortality to brighten your day. A mischievous muse must have seeded the idea to write about dying—not other people dying, or dying in general, but about *my* death.

What if I knew my time was coming next Thursday morning at seven? No bargaining, no conditions, no choice, no "but, but, but..." No. That's it. Already booked. No deals, no exchanges, no way out. Six days from now.

Really?

Yes.

This is it, final?

Yep.

Okay. I don't expect to, really, but if I'm to die next Thursday, there are things I want to do first. I have people to thank, people to forgive, others to apologize to—some of them all the same folks. I've letters to pen and stories calling to be written, a bunch of ordinary stuff I've been putting off, and much more that just doesn't matter. I'm dropping myself as deeply as I can into the premise that next Thursday morning is *it.* I accept the challenge.

First, I'll tell my wife, Pamela. "Hey, you'll never guess what I just heard."

"We should have bought those pre-need cremation deals when they were on sale at Evans-Brown," she might quip, before it sinks in I'm not entirely kidding. I tell her the muse's message.

One thing I'll do is stop being prudent about diet. How much weight can I gain by Thursday? And what does it matter, anyway? Heck, we'll throw a big going-away party and invite everybody. Pop that Dom Perignon magnum that Peter gave us and I've kept in the closet since I can't remember when. It'll be a hoot to host my own wake.

There'll be no time for big bucket-list items. No submarine under the north polar ice cap, no return trip to an African game preserve, no visit to the pyramids near Cairo or Chichén Itzá, or to Uluru in the middle of Australia. No Alaskan cruise. And not even one more day with friends in Vashon, Gilbert, Masonville, San Francisco, Barre, Levittown, or Cedar Rapids, never mind Valle de Bravo, Cape Town, or San Miguel de Tucumán. With so few days, I'll stay close to home. Time with Pamela at the Pacific and high on a mountain are priorities. I'll order dozens of gifts online, to arrive after I've departed.

After the parties and dinners, after visits from disbelieving friends and relatives, a host of phone calls and scores of emails, finishing a few essays (and getting going on this one), plus sleeping as little as possible, it's Monday. Three days to go.

•　　•　　•

I was a year out of university when I met Pamela in 1971. We were parts of a small but worldwide group of people whose stated purpose was *to assist in a work of spiritual regeneration of humanity*. What higher cause, what more altruistic or noble endeavor could we align ourselves with? We were going to save the world! For the first twenty-five years of our lives together we did little else. We traveled and spread the word, founded and led a spiritual community, raised our two children, started and ran a business, drew hundreds of people to the organization, and helped make tens of millions of dollars for it. But the organizational part dissolved for us a few years after the well-loved leader died. Pamela and I swallowed our grief and disbelief, grateful for each other and real friends, and set out on new life courses at age fifty.

And here I am years later still, my time nearing, looking back. No, *looking back* doesn't describe it right at all. Time isn't linear. It isn't sand flowing through an hourglass. Nor is the past *way* back, viewed as though through a telescope backwards—small, indistinct, and insignificant. I see time as an elastic dimension. Past is continuously pulled forward into the present, attached by a cosmic rubber band. Everything I labeled "before" is collapsed into *now* like a closing accordion with the air pressed from its bellows.

The old tale of one's life passing before one's eyes has some truth to it. For me, though, it's more like being slammed in the face by everything all at once. It isn't passing before my eyes so much as hitting me between them. I remind myself I asked for this. I invited it. I despair over past wrongs and slights committed, feel good about jobs well done, and forgive it all. Years condense into moments: a Cliff's Notes look at a lifetime.

How much of a contribution have I made to "spiritually regenerating humanity"? I like to think I furthered that grand mission a little. I've sought to be an example and encourage people I've touched along the way to be their best selves, and I'm sorry for where I didn't succeed—with them, and with me.

What kind of man, leader, husband, father, grandfather, and writer have I been? Do I leave a legacy of good? I may never know much about a whole lifetime's accomplishments. My own actions, yes, but their real effects on others? What is the value of a timely kindness? What scar may an ill-spoken word leave? Maybe it's a blessing I don't know many details.

Monday night I come fully awake in the dark, but not for any usual reason.

You're not taking this seriously.

It isn't a voice, but the words form in my mind, clearly, plainly, unmistakable.

You really want to know how it is to die?

•   •   •

I'm in bed. I know I am dying. I'm flat on my back, immobile. Rigid. I can't move. I try. I hear voices, but my jaw won't work to speak. I feel the heaviness of my body, like butter about to lose its solidity and melt into the mattress. I'm Gulliver held captive by Lilliputians. I'm Uncle Everett in a coffin with the lid closing. I am enveloped in darkness far denser and deeper than the obscurity behind closed eyelids. The voices are far-away murmurs, indistinct. I cannot make out words.

I can't even discern my breathing. Nothing moves. I lie in utter blackness, melted. The stillness is profound.

I'm not breathing!

Terror.

Oh, God!

And I wake up.

I gulp air like my lungs will never fill again. My body shudders, chilled in its own sweat. I vault out of bed to prove my legs still work.

I understand as never before: the human organism is hard-wired to *live*—to grasp every heartbeat, every breath, every conscious moment possible—until it just can't anymore. Then fear, and panic. Then...

I'm still here. *A dream*, I tell myself three times. *Just a dream.* But I feel rattled to the core.

•   •   •

It's Tuesday. The dream stays with me. Other memories rise to dance with it. I once watched a red-shouldered hawk snatch a young rabbit in its talons and alight in a nearby oak tree, where it devoured the animal. The bird pinned the soft furry creature to the tree limb with its claws and tore at it with its sharp, curved beak. The rabbit would not have been dead until the hawk ripped it open, but from the moment of its capture on the ground it looked lifeless. Did it submit to its fate? I've read of biologists' speculations that when caught by a predator, mammalian bodies can release endorphins that effectively anesthetize the animal. Maybe so. The bunny never twitched or made a sound. In the dream I felt like that rabbit. Helpless. Surrendered.

Pamela and I drive to San Clemente. We walk on our favorite beach and have our favorite lunches at our favorite restaurant at the foot of the pier. How many scores of times over the years have we done the same? We don't have to talk. It's a perfect day. Far offshore, gray whales breach and spout.

Not long ago I caught a segment of a TV program about near-death experiences. A middle-aged woman had been trapped under a capsized boat. She described her experience of drowning, unable to free herself from beneath the sinking vessel. After fighting to hold her breath for an impossibly long time, a calm came over her. She couldn't hold her lungs' contents another second. She knew it was the end. She related letting the spent air expel, and feeling cold lake water flow in to replace it. She blacked out. Her next memory was of detachedly watching her unmoving body from above as her son pumped her chest in an effort to revive her. Then she was in her body again, coughing and retching, but breathing.

My lingering death dream mingles with memories of this program. I know her chill. I share the relief.

Tuesday night the dark dream doesn't repeat, but at first light on Wednesday I awake from another, equally vivid. Whether a rabbit hole, a magic wardrobe, a wormhole in space, a stone sliding aside to reveal a passage, *portals to elsewhere* are fantasy mechanisms portraying inexplicable transitions. In this dream, my portal was a long, dark, concrete pipe smelling vaguely of storm water and with an opening so far ahead it seemed like light through a pinhole. Crawling toward the mouth of the long tube was arduous. When I at last emerged, I stood. I found myself in a woodland clearing in bright sunlight under a cloudless, perfectly azure sky. From the deep emerald trees all around the meadow's edges, people stepped toward me, first dozens, then hundreds. How extraordinary: I knew each one! Every face was unchanged from the last time I had seen it, no matter how recently or long ago.

Out of the woods on all sides came an ordered progression. Three Jims stepped into the clearing at the same time, the start of a throng gently surging toward me. Each one came up very close, face to face, and then *passed right through me*! I turned, thinking I could watch them come out my other side, but they didn't. All around me, others approached with measured steps. There was nothing menacing about the scene. It had the feeling of ceremony, a commemoration.

No one spoke. The only sounds were of birds playing in the leafy trees surrounding the meadow. Two men came near and I thought, "It's all okay," to George and Achal, and then "I'm *truly sorry*" to Patricia and Steve as they filed placidly through me. Here were my maternal grandfather, whom I never knew, and my dad and mom, and several Mr. Kims, Michaels, Richards, and Marias, Daves, Ellens, and Anns. In the procession were innumerable individuals whose names I didn't need to recall right then, though I knew them. They were Korean, South African, Mexican, Japanese, Ghanaian, and Argentine friends, their soft smiles surrounded by all hues of skin. Connections from the Americas to China, India to Zimbabwe, Italy to Australia— many were people I'd met and known while immersed in that spiritual regeneration project. Everyone flowed toward me and through me as I stood, still, in that woodland meadow. Last to appear were Lillian, Bill, Lloyd, Martin, Alan, Grace, Roger, and a striking blue-eyed man who didn't need a name. With each person who came I locked gazes, and everything that needed communicating passed between us in an instant.

Pamela wasn't part of the dream. She was asleep in bed beside me.

I'm awake now, yet the image remains as present as the waking world. Curiously, I feel emptied by being filled with so many people. Cleansed. The air is out of the accordion. A lifetime has not been miraculously resolved or absolved, but I feel every detail has cycled back through me and is put to rest.

What has a beginning also must end. I know that about my body. It will die at some point. I have an idea now what that might be like. Years ago, I at first believed, then sensed, then felt sure: I am also *more* than my body. I'm the life in it.

Like the drowning woman realized, I am human, and more. Human *beings,* we call ourselves. The human part ceases functioning eventually, but the *being* lives. The *being* is life itself. With serene clarity I know the first dream was about the *human* part. The second was about *being*. Both are true.

•   •   •

It is six-thirty Thursday—a morning like thousands of others, though I slept fitfully. Pamela and I sit on our upstairs deck with our coffee mugs, watching the light arrive from behind San Jacinto Mountain forty miles to the east. A near-white barn owl sweeps soundlessly over us on its way home after a night out. A small, rose-throated bird alights on the railing in front of where we sit. It cocks its head and looks sideways at us, curious and quiet.

I recount again the second dream to Pamela, about every-body who'd played a part, large or small, in my life. How the contents of decades can spiral back through in moments.

It is six-fifty. Seven will come and go.

I feel like a traveler returned from my two-dream odyssey. The morning's radiance warms the skin I'm glad to be in.

I WAS NEVER IN RONA'S CLOSET

Rona and I hadn't seen each other in over half a century when we met for lunch in Melville, Long Island, on a recent May day. We reintroduced ourselves, pored over old class photos, laughed and talked of teachers and classmates from decades ago, and told childhood stories.

Remember the time...?

This is one of those.

It's all according to Rona, who was there. I wasn't.

I was never in Rona's closet, though she insisted I was. So I didn't remember the time, but Rona did: June 1959, a perfect Long Island day, with cumulus puffs afloat in soft blue above, the lower world clad in early summer's luxuriant green. But the *most* perfect thing? Sixth grade was over! The next school year lay beyond a distant horizon, not yet given a thought.

Three twelve-year-olds, Jack, Colin, and Joel, rode their bikes on Shelter Lane, near their Levittown school. If I was there, I would have been Jack, but remember, this is all just according to Rona.

Colin's house was on Shelter Lane, so the other two would have met him there to set off riding. Often, and this day was no exception, it was with no destination in mind. Summers still stretched long and languid at that age; boys could bike for hours and still be home for lunch on time. None of them had money, save a few coins. So, much as they would have loved it, a stop at the soda fountain in the Center Lane drugstore wouldn't be happening.

Rona's house was on Shelter, too. Hers was a standard Levitt Cape Cod. These were cottages, really, with a centered front door opening onto a wooden stairway to two upper rooms. In Rona's house the upstairs rooms were shared by her brothers; hers was the smaller of the two downstairs bedrooms at the back of the house, next to the bathroom, and her parents had the larger. The living room was to the left of the entry, and the kitchen with its side door was to the right. Everyone knew their way around a Cape Cod. They were all the same. In the Levittown of the late 1950s there were few architectural anomalies.

Three abreast, pedaling easily along on the asphalt street, the boys spotted their classmate Rona in her front yard several houses ahead. She waved when she saw them approaching. Reaching her house, the boys turned their bikes in unison, bucked the curb in formation, and rode up onto the grass. As if performing a practiced maneuver, they hopped off their two-wheeled steeds and lay them parallel on the lawn.

Something magnetic was going on.

Part of it was Rona, of course. The boys all considered her one of the prettiest girls in the sixth grade, and there she was, standing outside her front door, beckoning. To the boys, she was a preteen temptress, a grade-six siren.

But it was more than Rona, cute as she was. Something stronger, deeper, pulled the boys inexorably, something twelve-year-olds—especially broke, male twelve-year-olds—are powerless to resist.

Food.

Rona's enticement wasn't just *any* food, though. Very near the top of the prepubescent nutritional pyramid, way up in the exalted company of cheeseburgers, cherry Cokes, pizza, chocolate malts, and French fries with ketchup, were pistachio nuts. Inside Rona's house was a stash the size of Staten Island.

How did the boys know this? They weren't psychic.

Rona had told them about it at school.

"Guess what my father keeps in the hall closet..."

A secret of such magnitude and import is uncontainable, especially among three guys with thirty-seven cents between them. In the store on Center Lane a small bag of wondrous red-shelled pistachios cost a quarter. That was a lot of money. And it was a *small* cellophane bag, with red, blue, and black writing on it, coated on the inside with oil and salt. Including the time required for the thumbs-and-forefingers shelling process, the nuts inside a twenty-five-cent bag could be consumed in ninety seconds.

So imagine how the mere prospect of a pistachio stash measured in *pounds*, not ounces, affected the lads.

Rona's father, Mr. Selsky, managed an archery and golf driving range in nearby Massapequa. One of his responsibilities was to stock the several coin-operated pistachio vending machines on the property. He stored the master supply of nuts in a weighty translucent plastic sack at home, on the floor of the hall closet between the downstairs bedrooms.

In those days, pistachios were imported from the Middle East, mostly Iran, though small print on some brands' packaging read "Persia." Iran remains the largest pistachio grower in the world; California didn't become a significant force in the world pistachio market until the late 1970s. Importers dyed the shells red to give the nuts a distinctive appearance and to hide blemishes. To American kids in the '50s, red was just how they came; it would be years before red dye's reputation was stained. You couldn't split the shell open to yield the luscious inner morsel without thumbs and forefingers turning red. Everybody knew what you'd been doing.

Within seconds of the boys' arrival, the front wheels of their bikes still spinning horizontally on the Selskys' lawn, Rona mentioned again the giant bag of pistachios, in case the boys might have forgotten. She also dutifully informed them that her mother was out, her dad was working, and no one was allowed in the house if neither parent was home.

Rona faced a difficult choice. She weighed the gratifying popularity elevation to come from letting the boys have something they really wanted—pistachios—versus the risk of disobeying her mom by letting them in. Evidently it never occurred to her to scoop a bowl of nuts out of the bag and bring them outside to share. Maybe she wanted to awe them with the sight of the colossal trove.

Her internal machinations lasted all of three seconds. "Come on in!" Rona smiled.

The boys scrambled through the front door after her and right to the pistachio closet.

Rona was loving it. She'd soon have them eating out of her hand. Grinning at the boys' eager faces, she yanked the bifold closet doors open.

There, at their feet, rested the heavy plastic bag, its top twisted and tied with twine. Joel, the strongest, could barely lift it. In the boys' experience, it was by far the largest quantity of pistachios ever assembled in one place. The bag was massive, and the number of red treasures it contained incalculable.

As a single entity, the three exhaled.

Their collective, whispered "Wow!" hung briefly in the air, punctuated by the sound of a car door closing.

"Quick!" Rona squeaked, suppressing a scream. "My mom's home!"

There's no escaping a Cape Cod except via the very door Mrs. Selsky was about to come through.

"Get in my closet!"

Rona hastily herded the three would-be nut thieves into her room and into her closet, closing the louvered doors on them just as her mother walked in the front door, packages in her arms.

"*Shhhh!*" Rona hissed at her closet, then a loud, "Hi, Mom!" as she scampered into the living room.

Mrs. Selsky wasn't fooled by Rona's overenthusiastic greeting. She'd just walked past three bikes on the front grass. She didn't need a flashing neon sign.

Feigning normalcy, allowing Rona a faint ray of hope that she'd get away with it, Mrs. Selsky said, "Ro, I found you a cute blouse on sale at Mays."

Having set her other bags down on the chair nearest the front door, she unfolded a white cotton, short-sleeved garment and held it by the shoulders for Rona to admire, her hands forming parentheses around the Peter Pan collar. A red-lettered "Sale" tag hung from the hem by a string.

Thoroughly distracted, Rona smiled. Genuinely.

"I love it, Mom! Thank you!"

She reached for the blouse, but the faux-grinning Mrs. Selsky drew it back to her chest and took a step toward Rona's bedroom.

"I'll hang it in your closet. You just go on with whatever you were doing."

Her nimble mother was already past her. Rona's excited flush paled to the color of her new blouse. *Trapped!* There was nothing Rona could do. She stood, her dark eyes cast down and slender shoulders slumped, as if awaiting execution. Even her cute bangs sagged.

Mrs. Selsky paused in front of Rona's closet doors, then pulled them fully open in a swift move.

There, among Rona's hanging clothes, stood Joel, front and center, too big to hide, his look of anguish and despair clearly confessing his guilt. A pair of sneakered feet on either side of him gave away the presence of skinnier bodies hiding behind dresses and play clothes.

"Okay, boys. Come out."

The three emerged, tense and wary, right into Mrs. Selsky's sternest look. Angry moms are fearsome creatures, and the boys didn't want to get in more trouble than they already were. Hands on her hips, Mrs. Selsky turned from them to her reddening daughter. The boys slid past her and made for the front door, still open to the perfect summer day outside.

"Damn!" Colin muttered as they lifted and mounted their bikes. They were relieved to escape the parental ire they'd left Rona to face alone.

"Nuts!" added Joel. They hadn't even gotten the monster pistachio sack untied before Rona's mom's unexpected arrival. They'd been caught and had nothing to show for it. Better if it had been red-handed.

Rona got a stern talking-to and a pile of family laundry to iron. Her mom let her keep the new blouse. She never found out where her father moved the pistachio stash. It became the stuff of legend.

•   •   •

Fifty-five years later, I took the Northern State to Route 110 and met retired schoolteacher Rona at Bertucci's, across Walt Whitman Road from the Melville Mall. We sat opposite each other in a booth for our reunion luncheon, and enjoyed seeing the kids we used to know still there in each other's faces.

Rona told me the pistachio story. "Don't you remember?" she queried several times during the telling.

I didn't. I don't. "How could I have been found *by your mom* in your bedroom closet, and not remember? And that mother lode of pistachios?" No. That experience would be right up there on my *most memorable* list of the era, along with a variety of significant adolescent firsts. It's not there.

About a week after the Bertucci's connection, I got an email from Rona. Her relating of the nutty closet event had reopened an old spring. Memories kept seeping to the surface.

"You know, I'm now pretty sure the third boy was Murray, not you…" she confessed.

Ah.

Like I said, I was never in Rona's closet.

Without knowing the power of words,
it is impossible to know men.

—Confucius

Educating Augustín

A Short Story

My name is Augustín.

Spanish speakers say it right: *Ow*-goose-TEEN. To others I'm Augustine—pronounced like the English month, August, with "teen" stuck on the end. To some, I'm just Augie. I don't mind. My big brother's name is Primotivo, and people have trouble saying that, too.

My family moved here from Michoacán when I was seven. None of us spoke English. I was terrified starting school, but at the same time excited to learn everything I could. I already knew *mis letras y numeros*, and I could print my name, but I could write and speak only Spanish words.

That was a long time ago. Now I have a university degree and a professional job that requires I speak publicly in English and Spanish. But when I was a kid...

There were other Mexican students at school. We would sit together at lunchtime, enjoying our familiarity and instinctively feeling safe. Our combined English ability was better than that of any one of us alone, and we supported each other in those early weeks when everything was new and strange.

The school gave us lunch. It was usually the biggest meal any of us would have all day. On a warm Wednesday a few weeks into second grade I was sitting at a table with my tray and my classmates. An older, bigger boy I'd seen around school was walking among the tables and benches. Maybe he was in fourth or even fifth grade. I was a runt of a kid, skinnier and shorter than most of the boys in my class except Paco, who still looked like a kindergartener. Paco was smart, however, and his English was really good, so we never teased him or called him *El Camarón*, The Shrimp, to his face.

The big kid stopped across the table from me. I looked up. He was right in front of me, looming tall. He pointed at my plate and said, "Are you done with that?"

I didn't know what he meant. *"Que?"* I replied. "What?"

"Are you going to finish that?" he said, his pointing finger now almost touching my cookie.

Cookies were the best part of school lunches. I always saved mine for last, and savored it in small nibbles. They weren't anything like the white, sugary *galletitas* we had at home on special occasions.

I couldn't make sense of his question. English words fumbled in my brain. He leaned forward, snatched my cookie, and walked away before I could say anything.

I sat, feeling something I would one day identify with words like "unfair" and "violated," but the only word I knew then was "no!" and it came out too late.

For the next two days I put my cookie in my pocket as soon as the cafeteria lady set it on my plate with her plastic-gloved hand. I didn't see the bigger boy either day. Then it was the weekend.

Weekends last forever when you're seven. If I could sneak out of our apartment early enough on Saturday, sometimes I could play *fútbol* all day with the other boys and not have to help at home. On Sundays I had to go to *la Misa* at the church. My mother would make me wash and put on my good shirt. Mass was boring. I would much rather be playing *fútbol* or running along the riverbed with my friends.

I never thought about school on weekends, and I quickly forgot all my English. But Mondays always came, and I went back. Before the morning bell sounded, the white-dressed cafeteria ladies gave us little boxes of juice with straws, foil-wrapped cookie bars with peanuts in them, and sometimes a banana. The ladies looked a little like the nuns at the *iglésia*, but were nicer. By the time I took my seat in Miss White's class I could almost forget how little I had to eat at home on weekends.

That Monday, the boy was back. I was holding my turkey sandwich with both hands and froze when he appeared before my lunchroom table. My stomach tensed, then flipped. I blurted, "*Es mio!*" but he grinned and took my unguarded cookie anyway. I flushed with shame and anger.

Paco leaned toward me and said, "*No hagas eso.* Don't do that! Don't let him take anything from you."

"But what can I say?" I stammered. "He's much bigger than me."

The Shrimp leaned toward me again and spoke in a conspiratorial tone behind his hand, "The next time he tries that, just tell him, 'Fuck you!'"

I didn't know what the words meant, but I believed The Shrimp had given me a magical English phrase to ward off my antagonist. The very next day it proved true. I looked at the big kid and said it, right to his face. The two words stopped the surprised cookie thief in mid-reach, and he stepped back, repulsed by an invisible force.

English is powerful! I didn't know any Spanish words that could do that. The Shrimp had indeed given me a great gift, a secret password to freedom. I now knew just what to say to anyone who tried to make me do something I didn't want to.

I tried it out on my big brother, Primo, that night. It stopped him cold when he went to flop on my bed. Then he laughed and laughed but wouldn't tell me why.

I was thrilled with my newfound knowledge. Suddenly I was absorbing and using every new word of English I heard, and my confidence with the language soared. Thanks to The Shrimp more than Miss White, I was becoming an English speaker.

It might have been a week or maybe even a month later when our teacher was about to organize the class into twos for a math lesson, like she did sometimes. I hated it when she had the boys and girls on opposite sides of the room line up in height order and then file toward each other to match up. I suppose Miss White thought it efficient, but I was always next to last in the boys' line, just ahead of The Shrimp, and I knew what was coming. I'd be paired, like always, with

La Enana, a short chubby girl everybody called The Dwarf behind her back.

I don't know what got into me. I was an obedient kid. My mother taught me to always be respectful of my teacher. But this time, when Miss White told the students to stand and go to the sides of the room, I didn't move.

"Augie?" she said to me, the only one still seated.

I didn't want to do it. I didn't want to be teamed with *La Enana*, who always smelled funny. I didn't answer Miss White. I just sat there.

"Augie!" she said, more forcefully, her whole attention on me.

What followed was the most important English lesson of my second grade—no, of my life to that point. I glanced at The Shrimp, who was looking at his feet, and back at Miss White. I wanted her to know I really didn't want to do the line-up thing and end up with *La Enana* again.

In my most respectful tone of voice, I smiled sincerely at my teacher and said the magic words.

Gourmet Gourmand Gang

The world had showered and changed and everything looked its best that spring morning. Pamela and I were to meet our friends Edith and Mark Anderson for lunch at a restaurant they enjoy and frequent.

It was our first time to the lively, casual bistro they'd been talking about. The four of us get together often; we're comfortable company. After greeting and seating and the arrival of an unrequested (by us, anyway) pinot grigio, we enjoyed a bubble of tranquility amid the surrounding hubbub, perusing our stiff kraft-paper menus. When Stan, the waiter, reappeared, Pamela and I each ordered the organic kale and avocado salad, mine with chicken. Edith and Mark glanced at each other, then looked at us.

"You sure?" Mark queried, the salt-and-pepper bushes above each eye rising on his forehead. "They have so many good choices here."

"Yes," added Edith, smiling. "You don't *have* to have salads, although I hear they're very good."

Hands in front of her on the rustic butcher-block table, Pamela gestured as she spoke quickly in support of our selections. Her preference for salad is sincere and genuine. Mine is semi-sincere and only moderately authentic. I mean, I like salads a lot, but there's more to life than green. Not that Pamela's vegan. She's never met a salmon she didn't like, and a good pork chop is sure to bring a hearty *mmmmm* from this Iowa girl.

Edith let it go.

Having noted our requests, Stan turned expectant eyes to our friends.

"The Kobe burger, please," Edith told him in a definite tone. "Medium rare."

"Same," chimed in Mark.

The waiter was gone in two strides. Out of left field I wondered if Stan was his real name. He didn't look like a Stan.

Our foursome's conversation ranged from art exhibits to concerts to movies and books, recent and planned travels, and, for appetizers, a few morsels about friends in common. We were into our second glasses when Stan returned and lowered a heavy circular tray onto a wooden stand.

"Kale salads," he said as he placed large, mounded plates of ornate greenery in front of Pamela and me. "Kobe burgers," he followed, with more enthusiasm and flourish. "Enjoy!"

Mark's tufted brows lifted as high as they go. He ogled the festivity that awaited on the oval platter before him.

I stared too. The full-pound (precooked weight) Kobe burger is a house specialty.

Nibbling into my verdant hillock I peered over my reading glasses at Mark as he positioned his hands around the four-inch-high mega-burger, readying himself to attack. What I could see without asking for a closer look, or a bite, was a thick charcoal-grilled patty slathered with melted cheddar, bacon strips, sautéed mushrooms, lettuce, and tomato slices, topped with onion rings, and stacked between but not fully contained by what looked to be halves of a small, rounded loaf of freshly baked sourdough bread. To tell the truth, that's the menu description, which I'd memorized. Now there were two genuine Kobe burgers right at our table. On Mark's and Edith's platters also rested embankments of garlic-and-truffle-oil French fries, each serving sufficient for a family of four.

I drooled on my greens. No one noticed, thankfully. They were busy.

The Andersons were enraptured by their lunches. In the nonverbal interlude punctuated by their moans of gastronomic ecstasy, I glanced at Pamela forking her kale with enthusiasm. Unlike me, she is immune to the tantalizing presence of behemoth burgers.

I compelled my attention back to the garden mélange before me. *This really is a good salad*, I thought, *but it's not, you know... I mean, it's not fair to compare... Just look at those fries, too.* If I'd kept it up, I'd soon be whimpering.

Lunch concluded with Mark winning the check and Edith inviting us to their home for a dinner party early the next month. We have each other over for dinner every few weeks, often with other mutual friends. Mark said it was their turn to host and announced they'd already started planning an impressive menu.

Theirs is a home where diets go to die.

Dinner at Edith and Mark's is an Event marked by gaiety and abundance to the edges of excess and often spilling over them. Always, it's a multicourse, over-the-top, culinary extravaganza. In our circle, the stuff of legend. To dine at the Andersons' is to be swallowed whole into a den of dietary iniquity. Just crossing Mark and Edith's threshold is good for an instant two-pound gain.

They start you off with unexcelled *Bon Appétit*-worthy hors d'oeuvres, sufficient in variety and quantity for triple their guest count. Mark graciously and repeatedly offers them to the eager, milling throng until the last is taken, as if there were nothing further to come. Last time, the Andersons served escargot in phyllo with butter-drenched garlic, herbs, and sautéed shallots, followed by a dollop of Russian caviar over Coulet Roquefort perched on a scalloped slice of Persian cucumber; these were nearly outdone by olive-oiled and seasoned tomato skins sculpted to resemble miniature roses. No chips and dip or simple crudité, ever. And no one's drink is allowed to sink below half-mast.

First-time dinner guests at the Andersons' can be lulled into gastronomic extremes before even being seated at their dining table. A perfectly medium rare beef Wellington was the main course last time, accompanied by Yorkshire pudding and numerous side dishes, none of which came from a Weight Watchers cookbook. And no one but Edith would describe molten chocolate lava cake with whipped heavy cream and Chambord drizzle as a "light" dessert. Her copious use of butter in nearly every dish makes Julia Child seem restrained. My Pamela, a dietarily disciplined Paleolithic proponent, shudders a bit behind her smile, but, really, we both delight in the indulgence. I more so. It's only occasional, after all.

For the Andersons, however, nearly every day is a dining adventure. Munificent hosts, they always put their guests in fine spirits with ever-flowing wine, stories, and engaging conversation. Their dinner parties can border on bacchanalia, but even well-wined we're all more than old enough to behave ourselves. Most of us have to drive home, after all.

An online English dictionary defines a *gourmand* as "one whose chief pleasure is eating," whereas a *gourmet* is "a connoisseur of fine food and wines." It differentiates the two this way: "A *gourmand* regards quantity more than quality; a *gourmet* quality more than quantity." By those simple distinctions, while Mark, Edith, and the rest of us are more gourmets than gourmands, we are all admittedly both.

It happens we're all boomers or better, and we sometimes privately wonder when our own mortality will start closing doors on us. In the meantime we've adopted Isaiah's biblical advice: "Let us eat and drink; for tomorrow we shall die."

All the men in our group have some waistline overhang. Once in a while one of us might say something about losing a few pounds, but our statements lack gravitas and credibility when made with a forkful of creamy chocolate éclair paused in mid-air.

The Andersons are living their dream. They worked for decades in successful careers and retired well and earlier than most. They fly a five-city circuit twice annually to spend time with their extended family. They feel they've earned a right to play as they wish, and they do. Some of us have similar means, others less, but we all enjoy playing with them even when it's vicariously.

For each of us, the excesses of younger years become riskier as we age. So what's the push to still go, go, go? Are we trying to get in everything possible while it's still possible? Trying to fill an unconscious emptiness? Desiring to share our appreciation for life's richness and treasures?

Maybe some of each of those, and more. I think of our group as nouveau-renaissance epicurean artists. Together we form a Gourmet Gourmand Gang, spreading joy and calories, and blessing the world a bite at a time.

Carry out a random act of kindness,
with no expectation of reward,
safe in the knowledge that one day someone might do the
same for you.

—Princess Diana

THE PIG

Cars used to be big. In 1973 we drove a four-door hardtop 1964 Chrysler New Yorker, a 413-cubic-inch, 340-horse V-8 push-button automatic gas hog. Our friend Chris gave it to us—he'd paid $400 for it, as I recall. The first time I filled the gas tank the big Chrysler earned a nickname that stuck.

The Pig's odometer had frozen somewhere well north of a hundred thousand, but the car ran well. It was a true road car—heavy, stable, smooth—everything our VW bug hadn't been. Though it was nine years old and of unknown history, that spring Pamela and I trusted the Pig to carry us and our young son the 932 miles from home in Phoenix to a church conference venue west of Loveland, Colorado, and back. Premium gas—the Pig demanded to be fed well—went for under fifty cents a gallon then. The Pig weighed in at an even two tons and got eight miles per gallon in its prime. When we owned it, it was past its prime and got maybe five or six.

Our son was not quite four when we made that trip. The Pig was so wide Broc could stretch out across the front bench seat with his head on Pamela's lap and his feet not reaching me in the driver's seat. This was the first time we'd taken the Pig on a long road trip, and of course we drove straight through. Forty years ago I could still skip a night's sleep and go on through the next day like nothing had happened.

On our way back from Colorado we were gliding along in the dark on Arizona Route 377, somewhere between

Holbrook and Heber. The heavy Chrysler ironed the road's wrinkles smooth as we went. Headlights illuminated the pavement way ahead until they disappeared into the black. We were lucky we didn't hit a steer or deer, but I wasn't thinking of that. I was getting excited. Home was only a few hours further, over the edge of the Mogollon Rim and down into the Valley of the Sun.

The comforting glow of the dashboard lights flickered and went black. The engine quit. Power steering and brakes died, too. I wrestled the wheel to ease us off the asphalt onto the narrow gravel shoulder, and stood on the brake pedal to bring the massive Pig to a gradual stop. Then it was quiet. Very quiet. And *cold*— nights in early spring are freezing at 6,500 feet. In the ebony sky over Navajo County, starlight shone through cloud gaps. There wasn't a manmade light in any direction. We sat in the dead Pig on the sloping shoulder, junipers almost touching the passenger door. We had no power, no lights. Mobile phones and portable Internet devices were years away.

Cold crept into the car. The wind was blowing—something we hadn't noticed inside the Pig—and outside was wintry. I took all the blankets and heavy clothes out of the trunk and made a warm nest in the back seat for Pamela and Broc to snuggle in while we waited. It was 1:30 am. Soon my wife and son were asleep, and I nodded off too.

I startled awake when headlights shone through the Pig's rear window. Our breath had condensed and glazed the inside with frost. It took an effort to open the Pig's heavy front door. A rancher was stepping down from his big pickup.

"Broke down?" his words fogged in the night air. Referring to Heber, about forty miles ahead, he said, "When I get to town, I'll tell the Highway Patrol you're here."

"Thank you!" He probably heard the relief in my voice even over my chattering teeth. My watch read 4:45.

We couldn't get warm again in the frozen Pig's cavernous belly. Pamela and Broc napped fitfully. I squirmed in the driver's seat, alternately snoozing and shivering until an officer arrived, his cruiser's lights flashing in the blackness like a Hollywood UFO.

"You need a tow." It wasn't a question.

An hour later, morning was yawning through streaks of pink clouds. The three of us sat in the cab with the tow truck driver; the Pig rolled obediently behind. The affable driver was also the mechanic, we learned. He told us his name was Bob, same as his shop. He had a pleasant, weathered face, not old, not young. He wore old jeans, work boots, a plaid shirt with rolled sleeves, and a grimy L.A. Dodgers cap that kept his short ponytail from flying around too much.

Coming down the grade, we could see most of Heber lying before us in the bright morning air; there wasn't a lot to it in those days. The tow truck's heater had been on for the whole drive and we finally felt warm again. The sun was rising through the pines as Bob steered into his shop.

"There's a pancake house just down the street. See it there?" He squatted and tousled Broc's white-blonde hair. "You must be hungry," he said, smiling into his blue eyes.

I think Broc was unsure whether to feel shy or not, so he just stood there.

To Pamela and me, Bob said, "Go get yourselves some breakfast while I take a look at the old girl." He didn't know the old girl was the Pig. I didn't enlighten him.

Nothing could have sounded better than breakfast right then. We walked the short distance to the pancake house, the sun now high enough to warm us through our jackets. Broc wolfed down a grown man's stack of flapjacks.

Back at the shop, Bob told us an essential portion of the Pig's wiring harness had self-immolated, reason unknown. He'd already replaced the burned wires, and he demonstrated starting the car. The Pig's V-8 responded with a roar.

Bob charged us $24 for towing and repairs, then reduced it to $20 when he saw the only bill in my wallet. We thanked him profusely, waved, and got back on the road for the final leg to Phoenix. A few miles out of Heber I noticed the fuel gauge read "full."

Our friends John and Carol welcomed us home. That afternoon I heard a whining, grinding sound when I drove the Pig three blocks from our house to FedMart for milk and a few things. I took it to Earl, our Phoenix mechanic, who could tell right away the front wheel bearings were shot.

"I wouldn't drive it at all if I were you. I'll give you a lift home."

Friend John, in a glass-half-full moment, reminded me that had a bearing failed while speeding on the dark road northeast of Heber, we might never have made it to Phoenix at all. Shorted wires made us stop, and the Pig got us the rest of the way home before revealing its more serious infirmity.

Within a day, another friend and member of our congregation, Connie, called and asked us if we'd like to buy her Toyota sedan. Connie was getting a new car. She knew we didn't have credit and couldn't qualify for a loan, but we gratefully accepted a ride to her bank where we all signed papers. Pamela and I walked out grateful for friends and Providence. Connie guaranteed the car loan, and we've had credit ever since.

Last June Pamela and I drove the same central Arizona route for the first time since the Great Fried Pig Adventure, as it came to be known after numerous retellings. This time we drove in daylight, and in a car forty-nine model years newer. Arizona Routes 377 and 260 look about the same, but in Heber, Bob's shop is gone.

Writing is writing, and stories are stories.
Perhaps the only true genres are fiction and nonfiction.
And even there, who can be sure?

—Tanith Lee

SOLILOQUY

A Short Story

I sipped my second mug of so-so morning arabica. In the coffee shop's kitchen, Ignacio whipped three eggs for my cheese and avocado omelet. The only other diners in the room were four white-haired and balding men spread around a table for eight amid an expanse of vacancies. They spoke loudly, covering for each other's hearing losses more than arguing their points. They'd finished their breakfasts and were on their umpteenth coffee refill. They were regulars—they fetched their own. If they irritated their prostates they'd just have more to talk about.

I held my comfortably heavy, white ceramic mug in both hands, peering over its rim to survey the fluorescent-lit room from my seat against the wall. A man and woman—a couple, evidently, although they didn't seem all that coupled—walked in. She could be late thirty-something, he a little older.

Flo, a caricature waitress if there ever was one, donned her well-practiced smile. Her youngish seventy-something face was pleasant and her dentures looked impossibly good. Flo's teased strawberry up-do had been sprayed in place since about 1962. I knew her name was Flo because I read it on her badge.

"Anywhere you like," she called from her seat in a booth by the door, her hand motioning the arrivals toward the dining room. Maybe she'd worked graveyard and her feet were tired.

Chuck—I'd already decided that was his name—scanned the room, his brow wrinkling and blue eyes darting, as if finding a table was going to be hard. Kristy was accustomed to Chuck's routine. They'd sit when he was ready—she knew not to interfere. Her face subtly paled blueish by her smartphone screen, she exhaled slowly as if she'd surely die of boredom without that device in her hand.

After about a minute—a long time when you're bored— Chuck said, "How's this one?" It wasn't a question; more of a general announcement.

Chuck's choice wasn't the best table, but it wasn't the worst. It was set for four, with flimsy stainless cutlery rolled tightly in white paper napkins. Like every other table, on its worn laminate surface grew an island of Tabasco, Heinz Ketchup, and Cholula Hot Sauce bottles, glass salt and peppers, white sugar and pink aspartame packets, and a little metal tray holding non-biodegradable mini-creamers, all overseen by a limp plastic flower. The daisy looked about Flo's age.

Chuck pulled up a wooden-back, green-vinyl-seated chair and sat down. Never lifting her eyes from the phone, Kristy shuffled over and did likewise. She sat on the same side of the table, to Chuck's left. Flo pushed herself up from her booth, using the tabletop for leverage. Without needing to look, she pulled two faded and fingerprinted plastic menus from the grungy rack on the back side of her booth bench.

I had a good view of the two and could stare at their three-quarter profiles over my mug without being obvious. Chuck drummed his fingers as if something should have already happened, but Flo wasn't yet halfway to their table after delivering separate checks to the old guys.

Chuck had kept his sandy, terrier-look hair the same for two decades. He was retired military. Navy. In the twenty-one years he served, he rose from seaman apprentice to chief petty officer. Now a few years out, he floated along on his lifetime half-pay pension and benefits. He was doing okay. He liked not having to work. Even his half-pay was more than his dad had ever made working for that moving company. Chuck liked that, too.

He was of medium height and build, on the slight side. If he were younger, you'd call him wiry. If he were older, you might say he was skinny. His jeans were baggy and hung loosely where his butt should have been. The faded salmon T-shirt was stretched tautly enough over his flat chest to show off its powerboat logo. He hadn't shaved in a day or two, but the scruffy look didn't add any Brad Pitt aura to his appearance. Neither handsome nor bad looking, his was just an average face, its only stand-out features those never-still blue eyes.

Kristy was past the years when she'd thought about children but had religiously prevented them. Now she didn't want kids and told herself she was glad she didn't have any. She could hardly stand her smug sister's three brats, although they were cute from across the room at Christmas.

Kristy's professionally streaked weave of blond-brown hair was tucked behind her ears and rested on her shoulder blades. A floral print tank top accentuated her frontal assets, firmly uplifted to form a fleshy crevasse. Her top did nothing to hide the modest roll of belly flesh just above the waist of her black stretch pants. Other than that little roll, she hadn't let herself go. Even this early in the morning she had her face on. The more-than-necessary eye makeup and arched eyebrows gave her a pleasantly surprised look. Maybe she wore it to mask her boredom, or to keep Chuck from asking, "Whatsamatter?" so often. It bugged her when he did that.

Kristy and Chuck got together about a year and a half ago when they met at a blackjack table in a casino out by the Salton Sea. Chuck was winning and his chips were piling up; Kristy took the stool next to his at the green felt semicircle. They partied most of the next three days at the Sirocco Motel on his luck, and neither had good enough reasons to part ways after that, so they didn't.

Flo minced over to where they waited. "Gitcha somethin' to drink?" she asked through her perfect teeth. She dealt the menus on the laminate tabletop, but they were too sticky to slide.

It was coffee for Chuck, Diet Coke for Kristy. For a second or two I played with, then dismissed, the possibility that Kristy wasn't her name.

Chuck studied his menu like a racing form. Kristy shifted hers slightly on the tabletop, then retracted her finger and unconsciously wiped it on her stretch pants. Flo ambled back with a white coffee mug and a sweating glass of dark bubbly soda, a clear straw protruding almost vertically with an inch of white paper wrapper still covering its tip.

Flo paused only long enough to glance at Chuck, engrossed in the menu. "Few more minutes?" she asked, but was already turning before either answered. Flo could read body language more easily than most people read a newspaper.

With some effort and accompanying commentary, the senior gentlemen's quartet arose in unison to leave. Soon Chuck, Kristy and I were the only diners in the room. They ordered, and Flo walked the handwritten instructions to Ignacio. Chuck got up and strode across the room, then out a side exit. Through the streaked glass door I watched him light up. Kristy broke her concentration from the smart-phone screen and looked up. For a moment I thought she might be looking my way, but it was an unfocused stare off into the middle distance beyond me.

Of course she sometimes wondered where her life was going. She never thought about deep issues like the mean-ing of existence, but she did sometimes question being with Chuck. She always came to the same answer. He was a good man, pretty decent in bed. She really liked not hav-ing to work her butt off for men who took advantage of her. Chuck might be a little quirky, but who wasn't? Kristy'd had her share of hard years, and it was really nice being taken care of.

Like that old song, she thought, "Love the one you're with." Things could be a whole lot worse. She'd been there, and this was way better.

As if called, Chuck strode back. Flo brought their break-fasts and refilled their drinks.

"Anything else I can getcha?"

"Nah, thanks. We're good," Chuck replied, eying his plate.

Glancing sideways at Kristy while she dug into her scrambled eggs, he smiled to himself at how lucky he was to have her in his life. In his years in the Navy there had been women, of course, but nobody he could just be himself with like Kristy.

Life is good, thought Chuck, almost loudly enough for Kristy to hear. She looked at him just then as if she had, and winked.

I'd told Flo I was in no hurry, so she'd taken me at my word and just kept topping up my coffee. Now I watched her disappear into the kitchen once more and return with a white oval plate and that black-handled, round, glass Farmer Brothers pot. Both were steaming.

Ignacio had framed the perfectly arched omelet with the grilled tomato slices I'd ordered. Yellow-green avocado was splayed on the cheese which he'd melted over the crescent of fluffy eggs. A sprig of cilantro crowned the creation.

With a practiced backhand, Flo splashed fresh coffee into my waiting mug. The aroma was better than I already knew it would taste. My full attention commanded by the plate before me, the coffee had become incidental anyway. I unfurled my paper napkin to free its captive cutlery. Fork in right hand, wrinkled paper in left, I wondered about the hands that had wound that napkin. I reached for the flatly folded clean one Flo, unasked, had brought.

"You enjoy, honey," Flo dentured at me. Her arrival, delivery, pouring, and exit were all gracefully completed in about ten seconds.

But in those seconds my soliloquy ended. The couple who'd been playing Chuck and Kristy left my reverie without ever knowing they'd been performing on my imaginary stage. They were freed to go back to being whoever they otherwise were.

Only Flo was real, and the omelet was great. I could have licked the plate. I paid my bill, left Flo a good tip, and walked outside.

The pair who had been my unwitting breakfast actors were out of character in the sunlit parking lot. I watched them climb into opposite sides of a maroon, not-new Dodge Ram pickup with California plates and a Salton Sea Casino bumper sticker.

Horrors

After boyhood years spent playing army, well after the cowboys-and-Indians stage, and concurrent with two-wheelers, Little League, and the beginning of the going-to-the-public-pool-without-our-parents era, childhood buddy Ricky's and my attraction to horror movies took root. This fascination was fed and fertilized by advertisements. *The Curse of Frankenstein will haunt you forever!* shouted the crimson-and-black film poster. We were ten years old. Of course we had to see it.

To the Meadowbrook Theater from where we grew up in Levittown, Long Island, was a one-mile walk, exactly. Thirty-five cents each got us into the art-deco-throwback brick building, but we also had popcorn, so the under-twelve admission price was probably a quarter.

The Curse of Frankenstein is a 1957 British horror film by Hammer Film Productions, loosely based on the original Mary Shelley novel. British actor Christopher Lee played the creature. Ricky's and my pulse and breathing raced for nearly all eighty-three minutes, and tension held us rigid in the Meadowbrook Theater's plush but sticky maroon velour seats. We knew if for a moment something terrifying wasn't happening, it was about to. Ricky and I both screamed when the creature ripped his own bandages from his grotesquely sutured face.

I don't know if *The Curse of Frankenstein* was made expressly to scare boys, but it sure worked on us. Ricky recently told me the bandage-ripping scene is still seared in his subconscious. The poster made good on its promise.

We knew movies were make-believe; we were suburban New Yorkers, worldly kids. But it's easy for ten-year-olds to forego rational disbelief and be swallowed whole by images on a giant screen. In vivid, gut-churning Technicolor, it was all too real to us. We were sucked all the way in, and then shaken to our skinny bones.

Eventually our tender psyches recuperated. Ricky and I could finally laugh about how we'd covered our eyes and watched the scariest parts through spread fingers. So we were ready for more the next year when *Horror of Dracula* played at the Meadowbrook. Of course we had to see it too.

For sheer fright value, the Dracula movie outdid Frankenstein by a mile. There was a scene where Dracula suddenly flew into such a fang-baring, murderous rage I felt Satan himself was coming off the screen to get me. I'll never unsee that moment. Thoroughly terrified, I looked down at my shoes for a few seconds—and there was Ricky, face down, crouching on all fours on the sticky, popcorn-and-butter-smeared floor in front of his seat. It felt like a long time later when we finally left the theater, shaking and scared spitless.

Good thing it was a matinee. Neither us could have walked home in the dark after an hour and a half of Christopher Lee once again menacing the world, this time with searing eyes and blood-smeared fangs.

Back at home after the *Horror of Dracula* experience, Ricky placed a small, plastic, faux-mother-of-pearl, glow-in-the-dark cross at his bedside to ward off a visit by Count Dracula. He didn't *really* believe Dracula would come in the night, bite him, and turn him into a vampire...but you never know.

These horrors sank into my subconscious, eventually forgotten but still present, dormant. A dark curse lives on in some unseen place. Dracula, though reduced to dust in the final scene of the movie, may still be out there—or *in* there. He could rematerialize from the depths anytime, even decades later, given the right provocation.

Last week, it happened.

Pamela was away attending her high school reunion in Iowa, leaving me a weekend bachelor. Early Sunday morning I awoke with an irritated, itchy feeling on the front of my neck. Over the next two days the area swelled and reddened while a hard, subcutaneous lump formed, about two inches long and half an inch wide. I ran a mild fever at night. Whatever it was, it wasn't improving on its own. When she got home, Pamela examined my neck and saw what she proclaimed to be two tiny fang marks in the middle of the angry swelling.

I went to an Urgent Care facility. The physician said the appearance was consistent with a toxic spider bite, but he couldn't speculate what kind. He prescribed an antibiotic and an anti-inflammatory drug, both with long, unpronounceable names.

A full-blooded arachnophobe since childhood, Pamela's worst fears were nourished by this event occurring in her absence. The very idea of a spider or nest of spiders or perhaps the mother of all spiders lurking beneath our bed turned her psyche to pudding. She called the bug exterminator company, but they were busy with everybody else's spring infestations and couldn't send anyone until the following Wednesday, by which time we could both be dead.

The thought of a spider hiding in our bed, especially the poisonous vampire kind, gave me the heebie-jeebies, too. I was glad to see Ruben, the pleasant professional from Home Guard Pest Control, at our door first thing Wednesday.

"Nasty," Ruben said, noticing my neck.

Was he referring to the angry wound or the perpetrator of it? I didn't ask. I followed him around the house as he sprayed along baseboards and behind and under furniture in every room. He assured me this treatment would rid us of my attacker and any of its kin.

Students of vampiric lore know vampires can transmute themselves from human form into bats, wolves, even smoke or mist. Now I wonder if they neglected to mention spiders...

Like the vampire slayer of gothic cinema, Ruben knew where and how to drive the stake. At the 99 Cents Only Store that afternoon, my eye was snagged by a small, plastic, glow-in-the-dark cross. I didn't buy it, but I'm having second thoughts.

DREAM CAR

Now, where'd I leave the car?

Not an odd self-query when exiting a shopping mall or ballpark and surveying acres of parked vehicles. But I'm not at a mall or stadium, and there aren't thousands of cars parked in neat rows waiting for me to remember if mine is in Section E8 or G6. I'm at home.

Where'd I leave the car?

Once in a while I rent a car I'd never buy, just to drive it along the coast or on a mountain road. I enjoy the drive, consider the rental fee an entertainment expense, and return the car, free of the payments, insurance costs, and liabilities that go with ownership.

I'm not talking exotic wheels, a Ferrari or a Maserati. Just something fun to drive. This time I arranged to rent a Mazda MX-5 Miata—you know, the cute little two-seater sports roadster. The hardtop convertible. Red, of course, like in the TV ads. *Zoom.*

But now I'm at home, and I don't see it anywhere. Only my 194,000-mile sedan occupies the garage. *Where'd I leave the car?* Outside, I look up and down our suburban street. No Miata. This is getting weird.

Inside again, I go upstairs. Our bedroom, guest room, grandkids' room, Pamela's office. My frenzied mind fusses, worrying. *Where'd I leave the car?*

Nothing. I look toward Pamela's office again. A red glint grabs my glance.

It's there! The shiny MX-5 Miata, top down, centered serenely in the eleven-by-fourteen room. *There's no way the car could be in a second-floor room. Is this a joke? A publicity stunt? And why does the Miata's grill look like a smirky smile?*

Where'd I leave the car? is answered, but I have another problem.

Ignoring my mental machinations, I get in the car, push the ignition button. The engine's powerful purr begins, and instantly Miata and I are on the street outside our house. And no sooner have I registered this inexplicable experience than I am waking up in my recliner in the family room.

Ah. A dream car.

I get up to drive my beater to the rental place.

Part of the secret of success in life is to eat what you like...

—Mark Twain

FISH STORY

On a rainy spring day in Manhattan I dripped into a Midtown deli on Seventh Avenue between Fifty-Third and Fifty-Fourth. I had over an hour before my appointment, and the delicatessen eatery had called me in from the rain-splashed sidewalk. I shook and closed my umbrella in the airlock entry. It was good to not feel hurried to order, swallow, and go. Most others in the bustling eatery seemed to be on a twenty-minute lunch break, though maybe that was just a normal New York pace and I, now long a Left Coaster, was out of step.

Avoiding eye contact, a vacant young hostess directed me to a window-side two-top where I could enjoy lunch watching thousands of legs rush by on Seventh. I put my raincoat, umbrella, and laptop bag on one chair and gratefully sat in the other.

I like New York City tap water, and that's what I asked for when offered a choice of Perrier or San Pellegrino. The trim waitress balanced a thick brown menu on the edge of the glass-over-cotton-print tabletop and had already slipped away when I looked up.

I could have perused pages of detailed listings of wondrous New York deli fare, but my scan halted at the simplest of choices: a tuna salad sandwich.

Haven't had one of those in I-don't-know-how-long, I thought. The flitting server reappeared as if she'd known I'd decided, and hovered the six seconds it took her to take my order. I gazed outdoors.

I wasn't in a hurry, but the sandwich arrived as if I were. I'd been staring through rivulets on the plate glass at the teeming sidewalk and street beyond. Umbrella-covered pedestrians hastened past each other in opposite directions, every one intent on their own purposes and destinations. Some performed quick lateral steps to avoid collisions. Dense traffic in the wide avenue beyond them behaved similarly, and at about the same speed.

I looked at the blue-rimmed plate before me. On it rested a thick construction of dark-crusted oval white bread entrapping a large mound of tuna salad. The impressive sandwich had been sliced diagonally, and the cut exposed finely blended white tuna salad standing two inches thick in the middle. Long dill pickle spears and a pile of potato chips completed the plate.

Mmmmm, I smiled to myself. *Just what I'd hoped for.* With both hands I lifted half the monster sandwich and bit off a large corner.

The tuna was really good. No, it was *perfection.* Without pausing to savor that first bite, I took another. The tangy taste and smooth texture colluded to spring the lock on a subconscious storage box. In it was an early lunchtime memory:

Boyhood buddy Ricky and I are sitting on concrete in the shade of the roof overhang in front of my garage door. It's a summery day, and we are little kids—four or five—picnicking from our respective lunchboxes while our stay-at-home moth-

ers visit indoors, a few feet away. My flat-sided, stamped metal lunchbox is a Hopalong Cassidy model, with Hoppy in a ten-gallon black hat enameled on the lid. Ricky's displays a smiling, waving Roy Rogers atop Trigger. Our moms have put cold milk in our matching kid-sized Thermos bottles, and we pour and sip from the plastic screw-on tops that double as cups. On the inside of my upper lip I can feel the rough threads molded into the cup's inner rim. Ricky nibbles creamy Skippy peanut butter and grape jelly spread on triangles of white bread; I have my usual Velveeta and Miracle Whip between Wonder Bread rectangles.

The Velveeta memory wasn't appetizing, and it wasn't what the Manhattan deli's tuna salad beckoned. Instead of rummaging in storage, I took another bite and chewed it slowly. The tuna salad essences in my mouth drew a resonant recollection to the surface.

I'd been to Jeffrey Feinman's lots of times before, but this may have been the first time I was invited on my own to have lunch at a friend's house. I was going on eight years old that spring of 1955. Jeffrey and I were both in Mrs. Daly's third grade class and in Cub Scouts together. We were also bonded as survivors of the Polio Pioneer vaccinations the previous year.

The Feinman home was a Levitt Cape. A chrome-and-yellow-laminate dining table sat under the kitchen window that faced Gun Lane. Through slats of metal venetian blinds the sunlit spring grass glowed Irish green. A humming Mrs. Feinman smiled, tousled Jeffrey's dark hair, and motioned us to sit down. She pivoted back to the kitchen counter to finish what she was doing.

I could smell the tuna salad she'd stirred in a blue ceramic bowl. An empty tin of Chicken of the Sea chunk-white-in-oil was next to the sink, and a rewrapped partial loaf of Silvercup Bread sat to one side. A mayonnaise jar had its back turned. The familiar rustle of a potato chip bag added a flourish, and Mrs. Feinman turned to deliver identical paper plates in front of Jeffrey and me.

She'd sliced the sandwiches diagonally, spread the halves apart, and filled the center of the plate with a small pile of chips. To one side lay a pickle spear. I'd never had a tuna salad sandwich in a restaurant then, but I imagined it would be served just like Mrs. Feinman's. I looked up and thanked her, as my mom had reminded me to do before I walked the three blocks to Jeffrey's. Behind her on the ribbed stainless steel counter I spotted a familiar blue-and-gray owl on the bag of chips. *Wow!* Jeffrey's mom had given us Wise Potato Chips, the oiliest, saltiest, best-tasting *pudayda* chips ever.

Neither Jeffrey nor I ever actually mispronounced *potato*, but there was a younger kid on the block who did. "Pudayda" was a neighborhood joke only third graders found funny. Mrs. Feinman didn't, and she requested we not make fun of the boy again.

I didn't think to ask her, but I learned much later that the special ingredient in Mrs. Feinman's tuna salad was kosher dill pickle juice. I wasn't admitted to the secret society of five-star tuna salad makers until I asked the waitress at that Midtown deli decades later.

And just like the deli chef, Mrs. Feinman thoroughly beat the tuna/mayo mixture to a fine consistency, and always used

Hellman's mayonnaise. At home, Mom used Miracle Whip, and she left the tuna lumpy, though she called it "flaked." Mom put celery bits in hers; not Mrs. Feinman. Mom's was good, but...

It's disillusioning to discover someone else's mother can make better tuna fish sandwiches than yours can. I didn't know the word in third grade, but at that age it's akin to heresy. But the truth was, Mrs. Feinman's was *a lot* better. My world wasn't very big in those days, but her tuna salad was the best tuna salad in all of it.

And it remained the best until the rainy New York day decades later when that deli sandwich eclipsed all previous records in my internal tuna salad rating system.

The waitress may have wondered why I left her such a big tip.

Bucket List Cruise

The Bucket List is a 2007 American comedy-drama film starring Jack Nicholson and Morgan Freeman and directed by Rob Reiner. In it, two terminally ill men fulfill a wish list of things to do before they kick the bucket. The term bucket list, *attributed to script writer Justin Zackham, has come into wide usage in American speech.*

I accompanied my old friend Jim Wellemeyer on a one-week cruise from Long Beach to Puerto Vallarta and back. It was an experience he wanted to have while he still felt well enough, before the cancer rendered his body incapable. In December 2012 we didn't know he'd die nine months later, but Jim knew his time was coming. He was already two years beyond the six months his doctors originally gave him, and was happily running on what he called "bonus time."

Neither Jim nor I had the money for a cruise, but several of Jim's closest friends generously funded both our passages. He and I were grateful and excited long before the *Carnival Splendor* cast off from the Long Beach Cruise Terminal. Jim had selected the line for price, date, and convenience. He was as enthused about it as a little kid.

Sunday, December 2

We brought Jim's wheelchair along in case he needs it, and find it expedites our check-in and boarding process. We have lunch onboard in early afternoon and attend the mandatory safety briefing on Deck 4. If there were a real emergency, Jim notes, the chaos would be total, so inattentive are the masses at the briefing. After trying on life jackets and straining to hear the instructions, we move with the tide of cruisers back inside.

We settle into rooms 2445 and 2449, Deck 2, starboard, aft. Jim watches some football on his cabin TV. His beloved Denver Broncos win; my favored 49ers lose—a better afternoon for Jim than me, but I'm not complaining. This is *Jim's* bucket list trip, after all, and he *should* have everything go his way. We explore the ship a little at Jim's walking pace, then have a quiet couple hours before our 8:15 dining room seating.

When Jim and I first met forty-four years before, he was the administrator of a spiritually based community and I was a college student. I was attracted initially by the philosophy but soon felt more drawn by the people who were doing their best to actually *live* it. Jim was among those I most admired. He was an unassuming man of sizable spiritual stature in my eyes.

Our assigned dinner mates at Table 356 in the Gold Pearl Dining Room are traveling companions, a lower mainland British Columbia pair, apparently enough of a couple to share each other's dinners but not a cabin. Manju lives in Burnaby, Mark in Surrey. He's a big guy with a ruddy Scottish look about him and a stereotypical hockey fan accent, eh? She's softly roundish, born in Canada of East Indian parents, with dark, exotic eyes and the kind of broad, welcoming smile you can't help but return.

Monday, December 3
I watch the gathering light behind horizon clouds, then sunrise on a fractal sea. The wave patterns appear random but

are subject to a larger organizing power, I note, looking down the ship's side from Deck 12. The macro-movement of the surface repeats its undulating designs down to the smallest ripple. Were I to paint this water, I would need a palette of black, darkest violet, indigo, blues of all hues, and some flicks of white for the foam. Then the sun skims the surface and I'd have to reach for warmer tones of golds, yellows, orange, red... Three-quarters of our planet's surface moves with this same pulsing fluidity.

I'll have an hour or two on my own each morning before Jim stirs. Today I walk the ship seven times, bow to stern; nothing but water and sky and beauty, unless you look around onboard at the dozens of other early walkers, joggers, and coffee sippers. I brave the crowded breakfast buffet.

Later Jim and I stand in the same spot where I started, admiring the vast, alive sea stretching to the edges of the Earth. Conversations and silences have always been equally comfortable between us, and we easily seesaw between them. Standing at the rail, high above the water, we laugh, sharing our recollections of how many times, back in my college days, he picked me up at the bus station in town when I came to visit his community a few miles away. The ocean before us symbolizes a far greater vastness which we each feel part of, a cosmic friendship we don't have to try to explain.

Jim says he slept very well. Whether due to his scopolamine patch or ample faith, he has no problem with the ship's movements. We're off to a good start.

It's an at-sea day, heading south and edging east, well off the Baja coast en route to its southern tip, Cabo San Lucas.

Sea and sky meet at the horizon in all directions. The ship is to reach Cabo early tomorrow and anchor offshore in the small bay. Tenders will carry shore goers to and from expensive excursions and the awaiting bars, restaurants, and souvenir vendors around the harbor. We'll be there most of two days, retreating to international waters in the evening and returning in the morning.

Instead of the free-for-all buffet lunch, Jim opts for the dining room, and we are seated with some pleasant folks, including Pentecostal minister William, his wife, and his sister, veterans of numerous cruises and eager to educate us neophytes on all manner of topics. The garrulous Pastor Bill claims senior "old-manhood" status at age seventy-five until Jim raises eyebrows by announcing he has him topped by ten years. Bill, a short, rotund man with a capillary-laden W.C. Fields nose, confides in my ear that he expects to meet his Lord and Savior long before he reaches Jim's age.

In the evening, back to Table 356 for dinner and our B.C. companions. We'll gather enough to write short biographies of each other by week's end.

Tuesday, December 4
I arose to watch the craggy brown southern tip of the Baja Peninsula stealthily approach under cover of darkness. It now stretches beside us, five miles away along our port side and ahead into the misty but warming sunlight. Jim and I enjoy breakfast as we pass offshore of the landmark natural rock arch and into the harbor to anchor. Numerous tenders—those small boats eager to take disembarking cruisers ashore—nuzzle the ship and jostle for position.

Jim is enthusiastic to go ashore. We ride a crowded launch, then walk through a *mercado* maze of vendor kiosks, most selling the same tourist items. The afternoon back aboard is restful. A semi-unmemorable juggler comedian show fills time before we go back to the Gold Pearl and compare days with Mark and Manju, the quasi-couple, who have done separate things.

I've been admiring the design of the ship generally, except for the décor of the Gold Pearl Dining Room. Paying too much attention to the latter disturbs not only my appetite but my sense of esthetic well-being. I'll just call it Barnum & Bailey Garish. After three dinners I've hardened my sensibilities to the gaudy, rococo walls and ceiling, and the god-awful carpet. After all, the table linens and settings are nicely done; the smiling waiters and numerous attendants pleasant, courteous, efficient; the plentiful dishes artistically presented; our tablemates more entertaining than they know; and Jim is happy. Hideous décor can be overlooked.

The *Carnival Splendor* is zigging and zagging a few miles offshore tonight, and due to return to the port of Cabo San Lucas in the early morning. The casino needs to be in international waters to operate legally, so the rest of the ship has to go too.

Wednesday, December 5
Déja port. We're back in Cabo under a cloudless sky. They say the temperature will reach eighty again this winter day. No need to go ashore a second time, we agreed last night. Looks like a day for lounging, reading, soaking, and, of course, eating.

While today is the same length as previous days, it seems much longer. Part of the subjective nature of time passage has to do with what you fill it with.

Mid-afternoon, while Jim naps, boredom drives me ashore after all. I enjoy a good walk on a beach of coarse yellow sand, after which I reward myself with a restaurant stop and order a local Pacifico beer. I guess happy hour is every hour at these tourist places, and *two* beers are delivered in a bucket of ice. "*Es la hora felíz,*" smiles the waiter. "Two for one." I suppose I don't *have* to drink the second beer, but it's cold and delicious, so I do. I waddle the rest of the way to the dock, board the next tender back to the Mother Ship, and take a short nap.

Jim has taken it easy, deciding to soak in one of the communal Jacuzzis aboard ship before taking lunch in the buffet melee on Deck 9. Last night we scouted and located the one he wanted to use, and this morning the intrepid Jim set out to find anew the hot tub he had in mind. Evidently it had up and moved to a different deck overnight. It's pretty easy to lose your way on a ship that's a quarter mile long with twelve numbered decks and stuff like *port* and *starboard* to keep track of, not to mention *forward* and *aft*, which sometimes unexpectedly become *bow* and *stern*. Oh, and *midships*... Jim eventually found a Jacuzzi and says he enjoyed his soak but not so much the moist interaction with a complaining hot tubby lady. And I don't know if he actually found the tub he sought; Jim doesn't either. The good thing is, no matter the adventure, he manages to find his way back to Cabin 2445. I'm careful to ensure he has all the help and companionship he needs, but also all the freedom and space he wants to do things on his own.

He is an independent man. Jim was past seventy when he acquired certification as a gemologist and began supplementing his very modest retirement income by selling pearls and semiprecious stone jewelry at swap meets and craft fairs a couple weekends a month. He isn't a pushy salesman; Jim really likes people. He is caring and warmly genuine with everyone. His clients remember *him* more than they do his wares.

It's about 4:00 pm and the *Splendor* has pulled away from the Cabo San Lucas harbor. We're on our way to Puerto Vallarta, an overnight away. Jim and I are on our way for coffee. He likes it, and today I need it. It's a long way 'til 8:15 and our next date with B.C. buddies Mark and Manju.

Tonight she refers to him as her boyfriend, but then they relate their independent activities of the day. Jim confesses his experiences of getting lost several times aboard ship, and I say I went ashore for a walk. Manju, we learn, is a veterinarian specializing in dogs and cats. Among other fascinating things, we now know that cats have clavicles and dogs do not.

Heavier seas tonight are causing the ship to pitch and roll a little more than previously. We'll be rocked to sleep.

Our late dinners preclude evening conversations. By the time we get back to our cabins Jim is ready to turn in. I feel he wants to talk, though; I've sensed this the past few nights. Maybe tomorrow.

Thursday, December 6
Jim is up earlier than usual. We stroll an upper deck and watch the sky brighten softly behind billowy mists. The

ship is entering the broad crescent bay that protects Puerto Vallarta, and the growing light has created fuzzy-edged silhouettes of the distant mountains.

We admire a dozen or more dolphins leaping and playing ahead of the bow. When they choose, they can streak ahead much faster than the ship is moving.

The captain, or a computer, parallel-parks the massive vessel against a long concrete dock. Jim and I walk down the gangplank, get around the milling crowd, and hail a taxi to the Malecón, a waterfront area with shops, clubs, and restaurants along a wide promenade adjacent to the beach. Jim buys a few gift items before we enjoy a fresh seafood lunch in an open restaurant with only the beach between us and the water. About a hundred pelicans are putting on a great show. We could easily stay another hour enjoying it all.

A restful afternoon of reading and relaxing precedes another fine dinner. We now know more than a little about Manju's dog and Mark's cat. If there's anything negative about the day, it's that the ship doesn't receive the channel for *Thursday Night Football*, but we learn later that the Broncos routed the Raiders 26–13, so Jim goes to bed happy.

We've left Puerto Vallarta to sail without stops all the way back to Long Beach.

Friday, December 7
Layers of clouds float below the blue beyond and above the blue below. The digital GPS image on our TVs shows the ship heading back toward the southern tip of Baja, but we're yet

too far away to spy it. Just some low cumuli clinging to the distant northern horizon suggest land's presence.

The sea seems calm for the open Pacific as we head northwest at 21 knots. (We know the knot-thing because it's on the TV too.) The high land of Baja is starting to emerge like Avalon into misty visibility, just ahead to starboard. Jim has gone to Deck 9 for another Jacuzzi soak. He'll find it. I hope he remembers to take his shirt off this time, and I wish him more convivial tub mates.

Jim said his breakfast table conversation today was dominated by a pleasant Minnesotan relating his near-death experience of four years ago. The man evidently did not have an "I am not my body" revelation as many do, but he's happy to be alive.

Earlier, I sat with a couple from near Cedar Rapids, Iowa—ample, first-time cruisers who kept looking at their watches and eating off each other's mounded plates. They said they were going to a salsa lesson and didn't want to be late. My imagination was streaking ahead to an image of this round couple attempting to Latin dance, when they explained they were on their way to a cook's demonstration of how to make authentic Mexican pico de gallo salsa.

The cabin steward assigned to our section of Deck 2 is Roderick, an outgoing young Filipino who spends eight straight months a year working cruises for Carnival. He won't see Manila again for five months. Each evening when we return from the Mark and Manju reunion in the Gold Pearl Dining Room, Roderick has left us towel creatures on our turned-down beds. Dogs, swans, rabbits, elephants, and frogs have been added so far to our terry menageries. Jim and I learned today from Roderick that "thank you" in his native Tagalog is *salama*, with accent on the middle *a*.

We are passing the Cabo coast only a couple of miles or so offshore. Here at the tip of Baja, the waters of the Pacific and the Sea of Cortez mix, creating choppy conditions. It's a scaled-down version of the colossal phenomenon off Cape Town where the Atlantic and Indian Oceans collide.

As the afternoon progresses into evening we move steadily up the coast. The cloud cover has thickened to mostly overcast and the temperature has fallen to seventy degrees.

Jim is pacing himself on this voyage, doing what he can or wants to, and nothing more. We've known each other a long time. He doesn't have to tell me he's happily enjoying the whole aboard-ship experience.

But I've been sensing Jim wants to talk since the second day of the cruise. Today, he says so. I'm the appointed executor of his estate and we've talked before about his will and wishes, and about our friend Alan and I speaking at his memorial service. Jim's affairs are in impeccable order, but I assume he wants to go over some things again; he's that thorough. We've also spoken before about physical mortality, and I've seen no hint that Jim isn't at peace with that inevitability even as it nears. I was with him in Mexico when he nearly died during an operation that turned out to allow him the better part of another three years. He isn't afraid of dying.

But instead, Jim wants to talk about his estranged daughter. This is not a new topic between us either, but I feel him reaching into the dark again, fumbling, trying to make sense of something he can't grasp. He's told me the backstory before, and he doesn't repeat it. He just wants a friend to sit with him in his sadness. Over time, Jim has accepted the finality of the severed relationship, but talking in his cabin now aboard ship is the first and only time I've seen my friend cry.

Saturday, December 8
Only occasional glimpses of islands off the Baja coast interrupt the unbroken expanse of sea. This morning, without blue sky and sunshine dancing on it, the ocean's surface is dull gray, like in an old black-and-white film. I have what may be a private whale-spotting: a single impressive spout and curve of mottled gray back quite near the ship as we pass like opposing traffic. Smart whale. She's going south.

Jim and I share a lunch table with three youngish women from Bullhead City, Arizona. Even after almost a week aboard ship, they still marvel aloud to each other about how big the ocean is. Before we get to know them better, they leave the table early to seek a second lunch on a different deck.

The gray overcast has thickened further as we continue northward this afternoon, and the temperature has sunk to just below sixty degrees. No Jacuzzi today.

At the final supper this evening we learn that both Mark and Manju have had previous unsuccessful marriages, hence their tentativeness about getting too involved with each other. They've known each other just two years, anyway.

Sunday, December 9
I awake remembering Jim's major abdominal surgery in that Tijuana clinic. His doctors said he had been to the brink and

back on the operating table, yet he recovered. Later, on the day we were taking him home, Jim displayed jewelry for the clinic staff and invited each to take something they liked as his gift of appreciation for their care.

We arrive in Long Beach Harbor on schedule, under a thickly overcast sky. We have plenty of time for a final cruise breakfast, seated this time at an eight-person round, including couples from Huntington Beach, California; Fort Lauderdale, Florida; and dual Minnesota (summer)/Arizona (winter). Out the dining room's aft windows, the stern and starboard side of the permanently moored *Queen Mary* appears close, now washed in filtered, pinkish sunlight. Our week aboard the *Carnival Splendor* concludes as it started: eating.

We disembark, the round-trip voyage complete. Jim checks the biggest remaining item off his bucket list.

● ● ●

Epilogue

Just about every school day my Pamela makes a salad for her lunch, tossing ingredients in a Tupperware container and snapping the lid shut before leaving for her subbing assignment. On a shelf in our little pantry, round and square plastic bowls of several sizes nest in jumbled array. One morning, her salad contained but not sealed, Pamela hurriedly rummages around for a matching plastic top. The one she chooses fits. I watch her fix it in place, and we both read the word indelibly Sharpied on it.

Jim.

The tumor in our friend Jim's abdomen had grown into a hard, iceberg-like protuberance. The thin, mottled skin of his belly stretched, straining to contain it. His suddenly aged body lay emaciated, sallow. Only in his eyes was his presence evident. The simplest actions required great effort. He said his time was close. He knew. Stage 4 cancer takes no prisoners, but for most of the three years after his diagnosis, Jim's quality of life was pretty darn good compared to many whose bodies contend with this insidious destroyer.

For eighty-six years Jim's zest for life, his open-hearted friendliness, and his steadfastness to his ideals never failed. Nor did his sense of humor. He wouldn't let illness take him out of character. Even in his final months, even after he'd seen the signs, put on his turn signal, and started down the exit ramp, he still did what he liked to do. Well, maybe a little less, yes. And more slowly. But he dressed as sharply as ever, welcomed every friend's visit, walked as much as he could, watched his ball games, read a lot, enjoyed his favorite foods, and even went on a few trips, including his bucket list cruise on the Pacific coast of Mexico.

"Not bad for a dying man," he'd grin.

Pamela and I were among a small group of Jim's friends who fixed and delivered his meals in the months before his final days. For years before, we'd enjoyed taking Jim to lunch now and then, and there we were, taking lunch to Jim.

He's been gone since September 2013. Now, Pamela makes it a point to use a container the "Jim" lid fits. Just about every school day, she takes Jim to lunch. We smile each time I see them both off.

"What day is it?" asked Winnie the Pooh.
"It's today," squeaked Piglet.
"My favorite day," said Pooh.

—A. A. Milne

BETWEEN

Today I have little to do. It's a rare kind of day, and unexpected.

For months I've been busy, busy, busy, working on and worrying about a big business proposal, which I finally submitted yesterday. I expect a response to come and negotiations to ensue, but for right now, I have little to do, and nothing at all to do about that project. It's as done as it can be, for today—off my desk and off my mind.

This morning I awoke to dense fog. The usual happy sunrise didn't happen—no red glow, no golden streaks, no mountain silhouettes to the east. The fog simply diffused from dark to gray, then gradually to white, until sunlight lasered through it from above.

I watched it all happen through the kitchen window. I absently sipped coffee, today's thoroughly read newspaper serving as coaster beneath my mug. Dozens of birds lined up on the backyard fence as the day lightened, loudly chirping greetings to one another and the arriving sun. Sparrows all, they shared a vocal range that made their simultaneous songs symphonious. After their good group chirp, as if at an unseen conductor's signal, they took wing and left as a single being.

How odd it is to have little to do. I feel I've ridden a pendulum all the way in one direction and now rest at the apogee, in that tiniest pause just before it begins to swing back. It's a most unusual and precious place to be, this space that both separates and joins what went before and what's to come, and yet is neither. Today I am *between*.

The moment of suspension between the swinging out and the swinging back is almost imperceptibly brief to an observer. But this morning I am *in* it—motionless, weightless, timeless, feeling aware of everything in this ethereal moment.

I want to stay in this place where busyness cannot claim me. My coffee's gone cold, the paper holds no more interest, the sparrows have flown, and my phone hasn't rung, not once. I sit, still, contained in contentment.

So what shall I do with all this time, all this space, while I pause between what's done and what's not begun? The moment feels full—nothing else could possibly fit in it— yet it's open, spacious, unbounded. I've swung out to the far point, and I know I'll too soon be returning into busyness, back into noisy life and work. But right now, I am here, *between*.

Time suspended, I carry the quality of the moment from the kitchen to my desk. Its magic envelops the space between my heart and eyes and my computer screen. I touch fingertips to keyboard to let these words flow out while I'm still at the apogee. I type quickly, concerned the magic will suddenly disperse and I'll be left staring at an unwritten page.

That doesn't happen. The magic persists as these words take form on the screen.

Pundits of many disciplines admonish us to slow down, to smell the coffee or roses or whatever that saying is—to take it easy, to savor the here and now. Wise as that advice is, in my experience it's not easily followed. Innumerable things vie for my attention all the time, each clamoring to be first in line. And there are the to-do lists I impose on myself, whether written down or simply worried out.　　•

This morning I received this unexpected gift—I think of it as a reward, perhaps, or a blessing. At the pendulum's apogee, however briefly, everything has come to a full stop.

Today I have little to do, and nothing I *must* do. Gratefully, I slowly exhale peace, at rest *between.* The everyday world will reclaim my attention soon enough, but I think I know how to get back to this place.

JA-DA

Words and Music by
BOB CARLETON

MR. EISMAN

Ja-Da,
Ja-Da.
Ja-Da, Ja-Da, Jing, Jing, Jing.

A few notes of that catchy century-old jazz standard and I'm back in junior high on a chilly autumn evening in 1961. Under the blue-white fluorescent glare of 1950s classroom lighting, I'm standing with other eighth and ninth graders around a blonde upright piano on heavy black-wheeled casters. It's Friday Recreation Night at the school.

Overseen by volunteer teachers, Rec Night was two hours of wholesome activities like basketball, music, wood shop, cookie baking, and dancing. I never baked cookies, though I ate a few, but I always spent the second hour in the library. Tables and chairs were moved aside to make space for the piano.

At the keyboard was Mr. Eisman, enthusiastically fingering melodies and chording accompaniment to popular songs from the 1920s, '30s and '40s while we clutched mimeographed pages of lyrics and sang along. Whether a handful of students or three dozen, we unabashedly followed Mr. Eisman's energetic lead. We even sounded pretty good at times, and we were always loud.

Long before he became Dr. Lawrence Eisman, head of music at Queens College, City University of New York, he was

Mr. Eisman, a young music teacher at Wisdom Lane Junior High School in Levittown, Long Island.

Mr. Eisman's unreserved passion for music, for teaching, and for kids is all the more impressive retrospectively. Though he was probably but a dozen to fifteen years older than we were, his infectious energy wasn't due merely to his youth. The man's spirit invited appreciation of music's methods and mathematics, its magic and majesty. All his students had to do was tune in to it.

I felt compelled to sing with him. One of Mr. Eisman's hundreds of music students of the era, I sang second soprano as a twelve-year-old seventh grader the year he miraculously led an eighty-kid chorus to perform the full score of *Porgy & Bess* with Mr. Dunbar's expert accompaniment on the school's sole piano.

At Rec Night singalongs, "Ja-Da" was a favorite, always sung once or even twice each Friday. The regulars eventually learned harmony parts, and we could really belt it out.

"Ja-Da" was a hit song written in 1918 by Bob Carleton. It's been a jazz standard ever since. In *American Popular Songs*, author Alec Wilder writes about the song's simplicity: "It fascinates me that such a trifling tune could have settled into the public consciousness as *Ja-Da* has... it's bone simple, and the lyric says almost nothing... 'That's a funny little bit of melody—it's so soothing and appealing to me.' It's cute, it's innocent, and it's 'soothing.'"

Ja-Da, Ja-Da, Jing, Jing, Jing.

Larry Eisman introduced Levittown kids to songs like "Ja-Da." Of course we listened to pop music like the Marvelettes, Del Shannon, and Dion and the Belmonts the rest of the week, but on Friday nights we fell back in love with songs born long before we were.

Nine o'clock always came too soon. We'd beg him for more. Mr. Eisman would look at the clock and at the door, smile, and choose another song or maybe two, and we'd go on, often until the assistant principal looked in from the hallway. Mr. Eisman would nod to him, and we'd finish the last song.

Only the best teachers have the kind of lasting, uplifting influence he's had on generations of students at all levels. His contagious enthusiasm at those Friday night singalongs, the fun we had around the piano, the old standards he introduced us to, and the joy of those times together, all bubble warmly in my memory. I don't remember ever feeling self-conscious singing with all the gusto I had—a welcome and all-too-rare experience for adolescents.

Now in my sixties, I suppose I can finally call him Larry, but he's in his eighties and it's still a little awkward. As kids, we were taught to address teachers and all adults as Mr., Mrs., or Miss, and I was a kid when I knew Mr. Eisman.

A few weeks ago, my elementary school classmate Rona (whose closet I was never in) gave me Larry Eisman's email address. I wrote to him, reintroducing myself by my childhood nickname, Jack. Within minutes I received a message back:

"Jack, believe it or not, I remember you. Not tall; light-colored hair... Enough?"

Of course *I* remember the skinny Jack Gray from all those years ago, but I was surprised he did too. I told him I wished to write this essay about those Rec Night singalongs. Larry Eisman kindly sent me some of his recollections:

"Soon after I joined the Wisdom Lane faculty in 1957, Flora Metrick's mother asked if I would give Flora piano lessons. Not a strength of mine, but why not? Flora was a good student and there were hours between my last class on Friday and Recreation.

"The lessons began, and continued until Flora left for Indiana University. The two hours included piano and music theory, and dinner. Then singing in the school library.

"I loved playing my favorite oldies and community songs like 'You Are My Sunshine,' and many more. I was particularly happy to see so many boys at the singalongs; there were always lots of girls.

"One side effect of those singalong evenings was my development of a style of piano playing which has stood me in good stead ever since.

"I left Wisdom Lane Junior High in 1962 to take a position at Queens College, CUNY, where I taught full-time until 2002. I still am an adjunct there. And I'm still in touch with Flora [who became a music teacher herself] and occasionally Rona."

I picture Larry rolling memories around in his mind as he wrote. I imagine him smiling, images and feelings blending contentedly. And maybe some minutes drifted by serenely before he typed this closing:

"They were the very best years."

Mr. Eisman, you made them so.

Ja-Da, Ja-Da, Jing, Jing, Jing.

Machinations

Cars, computers, and appliances are not sentient. Most of the time I'm sure of it, but sometimes I wonder.

Years ago Pamela and I had a very used car, a high-mileage 1964 Chrysler New Yorker we named "the Pig" for several usual and accurate reasons. It had been a fine road car in its day, but that day was long gone before we owned it.

One warm spring afternoon, the Pig started making a clunking noise. It got so the car clunked just about every time I drove it, but it refused to demonstrate the sound for my mechanic. After a while I started to feel the car was messing with me. Earl, the mechanic, smiled when I brought it in for the third time.

"Still doing it?" He didn't have to ask.

"Yeah. It's sort of a cross between a clank and a thud, but not a low-pitched thud. And the clank is a dull metallic sound."

"Can't tell what it is unless I hear it myself," said Earl, just like he had twice before. Earl always wore clean clothes and looked more like a schoolteacher than a grease monkey.

He didn't know but could have guessed the Pig's nickname. Earl dutifully took it for a drive. He sped up, braked, turned every which way, reversed, went through all the push-button gears, and drove over bumps. He did everything he could to get the car to produce the noise.

Finally he diagnosed, "It can't be anything all that bad if it won't do it for me."

Mystery unsolved, I thanked him nonetheless. Earl wouldn't accept any money. "I didn't fix anything," he said. A mechanic both honest and competent is a double rarity.

I got in to drive the Pig home. A grinning Earl leaned on the Chrysler's massive door and spoke to me through the window.

"You know how some people are afraid to go to the doctor? And when they do, they lie?"

"Yeah," I smiled back, knowing I was being set up for a punch line.

"Maybe this old gal is just afraid to go under the wrench."

Earl was still chuckling at his joke as I drove away.

I've wondered if maybe we'd hurt the car's feelings, or maybe it really was scared of being operated on, but for the rest of the time we had it, the Pig never clunked again.

•　　•　　•

Many years later I had a desktop computer that developed an annoying habit of freezing in the midst of routine functions. It wouldn't budge until I turned it off, waited a few minutes, and rebooted it. Then it might work fine for days before freezing again, but eventually, seizures would recur just minutes after restarting.

At the time I subscribed to an online computer diagnostic and repair service. It didn't matter that their call center was half a world away in Delhi. Someone always answered right away in a wonderfully thick Hindi accent.

"Hello to you, good sir! I am here to be helping you. May I ask what is your difficulty?"

Jawahar-but-call-me-Joe took remote control of my computer and I watched, fascinated, as he moved the cursor on my screen and went speedily through a succession of diagnostics.

"How long this difficulty you're having?" Joe's resonant voice emerged through my earbud.

I exaggerated my reply. It felt like a long time, and I'd had it with the PC's behavior.

"And you been having this computer how long?"

"Um, about six years," I confessed, shaving a couple off.

"That, I am thinking, is your difficulty. I would love to charge many dollars to fix your computer, but a new one will make better results."

I thanked him for his candor.

However, my old PC must not have appreciated our trans-global conversation about its fate. Just hours later, its motherboard flatlined and the hard drive halted in permanent cardiac arrest.

Okay, be that way, I thought, and headed to Best Buy for its successor.

●　　●　　●

Like most guys my age, I believe I know a thing or two about cars. Also like most guys my age, I'm a relative ignoramus about computers beyond what they show me on their screens. My intimacy level with appliances falls somewhere between.

Pamela and I bought a new side-by-side refrigerator along with several other essential appliances when we updated our kitchen seventeen years ago. Since then it has outlived two dishwashers and a microwave, but age has taken its slow toll on the GE fridge. It's still a cool refrigerator, but for years its icemaker has creaked, groaned, and emitted glacial calving sounds as it drops cubes into its plastic holding bin. For three years the door-mounted ice dispenser has intermittently gone on strike. Even when it would deign to function, rusty water drops would run down and stain the outside of the door. The bloody stains suggested refrigerator abuse, and Pamela hid them with black electrician's tape.

Before long, we and our closest friends were trained to not trust the ice dispenser at all. We'd just open the freezer door, pull out the bin, and scoop ice cubes with a plastic measuring cup. Once in a while, a guest, ignorant of our refrigerator's idiosyncrasies, would push the ice button, hold a glass in the proper place, and the machine would actually deliver.

"Wow, it never does that for us," I'd say, if Pamela didn't first.

"Does what?" the guest would query.

"Dispense ice cubes."

The guest would look at me with kind eyes, as one might at an imbecile. I swear I could hear the refrigerator purring smugly.

Pamela and I knew it was getting time for a new refrigerator. We had our conversations in the car, though, carefully far from our kitchen. We felt it discreet and considerate. Appliances are not sentient beings, of course, but still...

Despite our discretion, the refrigerator somehow learned we'd been talking about it. It knew something was up. I heard it strain to make new ice cubes promptly instead of waiting a couple days, and just yesterday we were again surprised to witness the ice dispenser work for an uninformed house guest. The refrigerator was gamely making an effort to postpone the inevitable, but how did it know? We'd been so careful to discuss the refrigerator's destiny out of earshot, or whatever sort of "shot" appliances have.

We think our Nissan squealed.

You may not realize it when it happens,
but a kick in the teeth may be the best thing in the
world for you.

—Walt Disney

NUMBER THIRTY

I slipped out of the house early, careful not to wake Pamela. I wasn't sneaking, really. She knows I go to Annie's now and then, and that I always come back.

Annie's Café is where I get my bacon fixes. Annie's serves thick, crisp slices of the delicious, addictive stuff. For me, scrambled eggs and grilled tomato slices are merely accompaniments.

What is it about bacon? I've read the USDA's definition—"the cured belly of a swine carcass"—but I never, *ever* think of it that way. I know people who don't eat it, but I've never heard anyone say they don't *like* bacon. Even my formerly kosher, once-vegan niece likes it.

On this particular morning, I guiltlessly savored the crunchy, salty smokiness delivered by one of Annie's ever-cheerful waitresses. I let the taste pirouette on my palate as I contentedly surveyed box scores in the *Press-Enterprise* sports section. But my reverie ended sharply when I felt a piece of something on my tongue—an odd, hard, non-bacon something.

I retrieved and examined the object. The realization surfaced: I'd cracked a tooth. More than *cracked*—fully one-third of a long-resident bicuspid had calved off into a sea of saliva. Luckily I'd already chewed and swallowed the bacon bite.

You can see I'm working my way into a dental saga here.

It's been a few years but I still miss my Number Fifteen, a molar whose demise I memorialized in "To the Last Bite," a true story of personal pain and loss. The tooth I broke on Annie's bacon was, I would learn, Number Twenty-Nine.

Peering into my mouth a few hours later, Dr. Kimmie began, "A crown, for sure..." That's actually the diminutive dentist's first name, and what the accomplished and outgoing professional prefers to be called. Many people find her surname difficult to pronounce.

"You know we've been watching its neighbor, your number thirty molar, for a couple years," she reminded me.

"Yes, I know." The periodontist, Dr. Choi, had declared the tooth eighty percent doomed back then. Now it's two years worse.

"I can put a crown on the broken tooth and it will be fine, but who knows how long before old Thirty here gives you problems? I suggest you consider..."

The centerpiece of Dr. Kimmie's recommendation for what to me seemed exotic dental work—judging by the cost, if nothing else—and the singular part I heard louder than "crown" and "bridge," was the death sentence she handed down on Number Thirty.

Her verdict: "It has to come out, and now's the time."

"Now?" I queried, weakly.

"Yes, we can have you out of here this afternoon, in a couple hours..."

I was to chair a City Planning Commission meeting and public hearing that evening, and thought it better I not preside as a numbskull.

"Tomorrow?"

The appointment was set. I was back the next day.

In the chair, reclining, expertly numbed and feeling the lower right quadrant of my face disappearing, I had time to ponder my long relationship with Number Thirty. The molar had been there for me for decades, and I'd callously taken it for granted. I felt remorseful. Hopefully I treat my human friends better.

I'd had wisdom teeth surgically extracted when I was a teenager, but my only awake experience of a tooth removal was that of the painful Number Fifteen. Dental professionals had *tsk*ed over that molar for twenty-five years, regularly warning me, "Someday you'll lose that tooth."

But Number Thirty's execution-by-extraction was to be carried out less than twenty-four hours after sentencing. No time to adjust. No years on Death Row. No long goodbyes. And Number Thirty didn't even hurt.

Dr. Kimmie returned and tested my numbness with a poking tool.

"Did that hurt?"

"No." I slurred the word like I'd had several tequila shots.

"Good! Let's get going."

An impressive array of implements were delivered on a tray. After a glance at what looked to be really big stainless steel pliers, I closed my eyes.

Dr. Kimmie went right at it with her heavy equipment. I imagined jack hammers, pry bars, backhoes, and cranes working feverishly to excavate Number Thirty. The molar resisted, its roots clinging to my mandible for all they were worth. Dr. Kimmie redoubled her efforts. Being all of five feet tall, she rose from her rolling stool and stood to secure greater leverage. She finally resorted to sawing the recalcitrant Number Thirty into pieces and prying each little chunk from my unfeeling jaw. At least that's what I imagined her doing; I couldn't ask. When the last of Number Thirty was extricated I pictured a bloody gum pit I was by then sure reached to my sternum.

But it was over.

For a while, Dr. Kimmie's assistants kept irrigating, suctioning, and pressing gauze into the new crater; then another specialist arrived to fit a temporary crown-bridge in place. Ninety minutes from local anesthesia to *adios,* and I was efficiently on my way, pain killer prescription in my grip.

A week's gone by since. Everything seems okay to me, but the thorough Dr. Kimmie wants to take a follow-up look next week. It will be several weeks more before I'm given the permanent crown-bridge, guaranteed for lifetime service.

I can hardly wait. Already, I hear bacon's siren call, and Annie's beckons.

LA SORPRESA

Acapulco. Sunny Pacific state of Guerrero. Rocky cliffs, piña coladas, parrots, clear sandy beaches, *palapas*, coconut palms, iguanas, tourists.

In the latter 1990s this was home to my longtime friend Eric and his wife, Tina. They lived in the left half of a two-unit condo she owned. It didn't have an ocean view, but it was a very nice place. Afternoon sea breezes would reach the second-floor bedrooms and gradually lift the day's heat from the concrete building.

The condo was halfway up a sloping street that paralleled a deep *barranca*. In the rainy season, the ravine flooded with roiling, brown water in a hurry to reach the sea. In calmer times its lush greenery hid most of the trash littering its jagged bottom, until the rains came again and flushed it out.

From the street, a spreading, fruit-laden mango tree identified Eric and Tina's driveway entrance. The day I arrived, two iguanas lazed on its lower limbs. I wouldn't have noticed them had my taxi driver not pointed them out after handing me my luggage. Iguanas' coloring camouflages them well. These docile, omnivorous lizards can grow to six feet long, but the two in the mango tree were less than half that size.

Tina was away in Mexico City when I arrived from the Aca airport. Eric and I, as always in our reunions, greeted one another with smiles, hugs, and manly backslaps. Before my bags were in the door, tops were popped off icy Negra Modelos. *"Chin-chin!"* the locals say when toasting one another. The term is said to represent the sound of glasses clinking.

Over our three-decade-plus friendship, Eric and I spent hundreds of days together in person. We traveled, worked, played, lived, ate, and drank together in times both easy and hard and in places from Argentina to Canada. I knew each of his wives and some of his in-betweens, and he knew my Pamela. We first met him when very pregnant Pamela was days from giving birth to our daughter, Melissa, in the spring of 1978.

Eric was born in Uruguay and raised a carnivore. When the taxi dropped me off at the Acapulco condo, irregular chunks of homemade charcoal were already whitening in the grill near the pool. Eric peeled plastic wrap from a wooden bowl and proudly showed me a mass of unidentifiable red meat marinating in lime juice, *chile*, garlic, red wine, and secret condiments. He must have read my face as he took a long drag on his filterless cigarette and, with a raspy, smoke-soaked chuckle, assured me it was beef. *No te preocupes, viejo.* Don't worry, old man.

Eric drew a large knife from the leather sheath he wore on his belt at the small of his back. He pinched an edge of the meat in the bowl and, with a single motion, sliced a piece off.

"Nahuél!" he called.

Eric's white, broad-faced pit bull materialized at his feet, tail wagging, ears erect. He gently took from Eric's fingers the proffered gift, gulped it, and licked red drops from the brick patio. Eric scratched him behind his massive head. Like all his dogs through the years, Nahuél was well-trained and obedient.

For that, I was grateful. Although we'd just met, Nahuél seemed to know I was his master's friend and not a threat. Still, it took me a little time to feel at ease around the powerfully muscular thirty-kilo canine.

In lingering twilight Eric forked the perfectly blackened, medium-rare meat from the grill. We sat at a small table by the pool to enjoy an unrushed repast. The nondescript beef on the cutting board looked sufficient for a good-sized family, but in a slow-paced hour it was gone. Nahuél had a few bites, and I ate a fourth of it. A nice Cabernet complemented our savory feast as darkness thickened around us. Eric and I randomly meandered between English and Spanish, getting caught up, but ours was the sort of friendship also fully at ease in silence.

I'm customarily an early riser, but the next morning, when I came downstairs and emerged into the damp, predawn air, Eric had already made coffee. I joined him at the table where we'd spent hours the night before. He poured me a mug of muddy Chiapas infusion.

"*Buenos días*," we said in unison, then smiled and sat back to sip our coffees and enjoy the day's arrival.

After a space of caffeinated contemplation, Eric rose and moved in his mildly bowlegged shuffle through the open front door and into the house. His flip-flops slapped softly with each step across the tile floor, then changed rhythm as he started up the concrete stairs. On the second floor were his and Tina's room, mine, and a bathroom.

What came next couldn't have been written true without Eric's later account, of course. This is how it went that summery morning:

Eric went into the upstairs bathroom. Seated, but before fulfilling his mission, he felt something. It was but the barest hint of a something, but it was a disconcerting something because the sensation was on his suspended nether parts.

Acapulco is known for its impressive cockroaches. They're ubiquitous. These dark red-brown prehistoric insects can be three inches long. They can fly. It was a logical assumption for Eric to make.

"Damn *cucarachas*," he muttered aloud to himself.

Prior to my arrival he'd dosed the house with an insecticide no longer obtainable north of the border. Marauding roaches were supposed to have been warded off, at least for the duration of my stay. Gringos typically have low to extremely low tolerance for the creatures, but to a macho Latino, *cucarachas* are simply part of normal life. Seated, undaunted, Eric lit another cigarette and resumed coaxing his objective.

The next thing he felt wasn't a subtle brush of wing, feeler, or tiny, scratchy leg. It was a *bump*. No, more than a bump—a definite, blunt, forceful *poke* from below.

Eric flew from the seat, turned, and glared into the toilet.

"Chinga tu madre!" he bellowed, more than loudly enough for me to hear clearly downstairs, outside. It was probably loud enough to startle neighbors, too.

The bathroom door banged open. Eric turned and yelled down the stairs, "Nahuél!" his voice booming.

Nahuél sprang to his feet and skidded to the foot of the stairs, his paws struggling for purchase on the smooth tile. He'd been taught not to go upstairs, and he obediently hesitated. But Eric called again, and Nahuél was on the second floor in three bounds. Eric steered the excited pit bull into the bathroom and yanked the door shut with a slam. Eric stood outside the door, pulling his shorts up.

His yells had rocketed me from my sedentary spot too, but Nahuél was much faster to Eric's rescue. When I reached the second floor, the noise and commotion from behind the bathroom door reached a zenith—nonstop primal growling and scratching, thuds, and a final, eerie, muffled howl. Then it was quiet.

"Nahuél!" Eric said softly but firmly in his command voice. The dog must have frozen in response. Eric opened the door.

We looked in. The toilet seat lay askew. Blood and gore smeared the porcelain, the tile floor, and the back wall. The shower curtain was in a heap in the stall. And there stood a panting Nahuél with the remains of an iguana clenched in his jaws and hanging to the floor. The reptile never had a chance.

Later we speculated the lizard had been wandering the condo's flat roof, ventured down a vertical sewer vent pipe, couldn't back out, and then found an escape route through the toilet. The poke in the privates that had so shaken Eric had come from the iguana's bony snout. Eric was fortunate not to have been clawed—or bitten.

For all the years that remained to my *buen amigo*, whenever we were together we'd laugh again about the gay iguana and *la sorpresa del abajo*—Eric's alarming "surprise from below."

For youth, everything is sport.

—Leonardo Da Vinci

ONCE A GIRL

The first social event of my wholly new life after elementary school was a costume dance. It was October 1959, seven months before I'd turn thirteen. My first dance at Wisdom Lane Junior High in Levittown, Long Island, was held before Halloween, but the theme wasn't ghoulish. It was "Come as something else."

I don't remember if it was my idea or hers—mine, I think—but my sister, Judy, dressed me as a girl so convincingly I emerged alien even to myself. She wrapped and pinned my short hair in a stylish head scarf like a movie star, my front locks just long enough to form trendy bangs, held in place by half a can of Aqua Net. I wore a tight, short-sleeved pink sweater over a bra Judy had stuffed with tissues and cotton balls; a long skirt concealed my calf muscles and the boyish scar on my right shin. I wore a pair of Judy's flats, which I kept walking out of until I caught on to the requisite technique of scrunching and relaxing my toes with each step.

My sister is three years older than me. I was twelve, she was fifteen, and when she looked at me it was from across the Grand Canyon of Puberty. We were on opposite rims. I think she had a great time dolling me up like Marilyn or Liz.

"You really want to do this?" she asked as she began assembling her array of secret tools and supplies.

"Sure. It'll be fun."

I *wasn't* sure, actually. I *hoped* it would be fun. Judy began her task of making me unrecognizable, gaining enthusiasm as she worked.

I was at the "pretty boy" stage of slender, pre-pubescent adolescence. I sat on a stool in the bathroom, facing my sister, my back to the mirrored medicine chest on the wall above the sink. She described what she was doing as she did it. Hair spray, light foundation, rouge, and lipstick preceded the most transformative magic: eye makeup. Brow pencil, eyelash curler, mascara, eye liner, shadow, extra corner touches that changed the shape of my eyes... I was surprised how long it took! Then small, clip-on earrings that pinched when she put them on and kept hurting as I wore them. What girls go through! She wouldn't let me turn to the mirror until she'd completed her alchemy.

"Okay. You're ready. You look great!"

I stood, turned, and wondered who that was in the mirror.

It was a shocker! I was equally delighted and terrified to be going to the first dance of junior high as somebody else. And I *really was* somebody else; the transformation was thorough. If I didn't talk I wouldn't give my identity away even to my friends, so I resolved to remain mute.

Thankfully, my dad wasn't home, and I slipped out the front door without Mom seeing me—I think. I started shuffling the three blocks to school in my unfamiliar footwear, getting the hang of it. It was still early but already dark. I scurried along as quickly as I could: scrunch, step, relax; scrunch, step, relax.

In a crowd of chattering fellow seventh-grade neophytes I scrunched-stepped-relaxed into Wisdom Lane's all-purpose room. Even my own teachers asked me who I was. I just smiled. The phys ed teacher serving punch in small Dixie cups, a man I realize now was probably all of twenty-five, openly ogled me. I instinctively looked away and down, then peeked sideways at him, feeling uncomfortable without knowing why. I learned later I'd given him an openly flirtatious look. But what did I know? I was an innocent boy inside. I'd never been a girl before. I couldn't see me. I didn't know what was going on, on either side of the strange interchange with the gym teacher.

Judy explained it to me later. The word *hot* wasn't in our vocabulary then, but I understood the concept. I would understand it better in a few years. She'd made me up to look more like sixteen than twelve. I was attractive, and though my burgeoning bosom consisted solely of stuffing, I appeared more perfectly endowed than any real seventh-grade girl in the history of the school.

Over the scratchy sound system came Ricky Nelson's "Lonesome Town." The Platters harmonized "Smoke Gets in Your Eyes." Most of the kids stood around in various degrees of awkwardness, talking, staring, lying about how good the punch was. I had no intention of actually dancing. Almost no seventh-grade boys I knew would voluntarily dance. Of course, I was still thinking as a boy, *but I wasn't one.*

Not recognizing me as *me*, a group of popular real girls swept me into their group cha-cha to "Venus." I didn't know how to cha-cha. I swayed awkwardly to the music a little, but I couldn't even fake cha-cha steps for more than a bar of Frankie Avalon's song. I had to escape!

I feigned a foot injury, wincing as convincingly as I could, and limped to one of the gray metal Samsonite folding chairs lining the room's perimeter. Both feet were actually tired, and I was glad to sit down while the girls cha-cha-ed on. I couldn't tell and never knew if they were just finished pulling both my legs, or if they were as genuinely indifferent as they looked.

Students' attempts to come to the dance "as someone else" had varied success. Most boys had outfitted themselves as banal versions of cowboys, hobos, or soldiers, and there were several Elvis mimics. A cardboard-and-foil robot (one way to get out of dancing) drew special attention. My friend Bob came in his Wisdom Lane gym outfit, probably a creative act of last-minute desperation. Some of the girls dressed as gypsies, but the most ubiquitous female attire was a poodle skirt and white blouse. The skirts were gray, the poodle appliques pink with ribbons—a popular Sandra Dee or Annette Funicello look. No matter the costume, however—even the robot—the *person* in it was readily identifiable. Except for me.

I shuffled my way through a mixed crowd of dancers (girls) and mill-around-ers (boys), headed for the punch table, relieved that Miss Brady, my English teacher, had replaced Mr. Phys-Ed at the ladle.

I didn't make it all the way to Miss Brady. Ritchie Valens's "Donna" filled the all-purpose room's warming, humid air. I felt a tap on my right shoulder and was gently but firmly spun clockwise, right into the arms of an eighth-grade boy!

Whoa! Wait! This can't be happening! I'm dancing backwards with a boy! I blanched, dropped my arms, rotated out of his light embrace, and headed for the open double door to the hallway. I needed to become invisible. I briskly scrunched-stepped-relaxed toward the boys' room, without thinking. Miss Brady's quizzical stare followed me.

I almost went in. A startled boy coming out looked me right in the eyes and nodded to his left, indicating the direction of the girls' room.

But I couldn't go in the girls' room—I just couldn't. Being dressed as a girl was now bad enough, but being subtly hit on by a gym teacher, and dancing, even for a few seconds, with a boy, were almost more than I could manage. I couldn't bring myself to sneak into a girl's toilet stall, and I certainly couldn't go into the boys' room, stand in front of a urinal, and hike up my skirt.

There was nowhere to go but home. I'd leave early, well before the Friday evening dance officially ended at 8:30. Although fooling people was kind of fun, the novelty of being a girl had evaporated, replaced by an increasingly unbearable weirdness. After remembering what I was looking for, I found my sister's jacket in the cloakroom.

Scrunch, step, relax, I exited the sweaty school into the cool October evening, happy to feel the parking lot's beady asphalt through the flats' paper-thin soles. Rounding the building corner in the semi-dark, I nearly bumped into a noisy, joking-and-smoking gaggle of older kids. I altered course as deftly as the flats allowed and was about to break clear on the long path across the school field—*scrunch, step, relax; scrunch, step, relax*—when I was roughly groped from behind by a boy I didn't know.

"What the...?" he growled near my ear with smoky breath. Then he laughed, turned, and shouted back to the gaggle, "It's a boy!" his voice cracking.

I kept going. To my supreme relief, I wasn't followed. He had grabbed, squeezed, and pulled on my left endowment, shifting one pseudo-boob to my armpit and the other to my sternum. I forgot all about the "relax" phase of the flat-walking process and hurried on, trying without success to adjust my bra, stepping as quickly as I could with permanently scrunched toes.

I reached home so early Judy hadn't yet gone out with her friends. *Whew!* She was in the bathroom, door slightly ajar, doing to her own face what she'd done earlier to mine. I barged in.

Seeing my uni-breast protruding from the center of her pink sweater, she let out a loud "Ha!" and began giggling so hard she had to sit down on the edge of the bathtub. When she recovered, my truly helpful sister painstakingly introduced me to the wonders of cold cream. I watched as she restored me to boyhood, very glad to see my familiar, though reddened, countenance reappear from under layers of disguise.

I was once a girl for two hours, a mystifying sojourn in a foreign land.

I made it back, and didn't even lose an earring.

Revenge is a dish that tastes best when served cold.

—Mario Puzo, *The Godfather*

RED END

For twenty-seven chapters the diabolical bad guy stayed in the shadows, hid among innocents, eluded discovery. Now our heroine had him in her sights. The future of the Free World hung on her trigger finger.

Spy thrillers are only occasional condiments in my reading diet. But a friend had given me the novel and I'd promised to read it. I kept it beside my chair to pick up, I admit, only when there was nothing else. I poured a glass of fine pinot noir and got back into it. The final chapter lay but pages ahead. It's hard to follow plot twists down dark alleys when you read only several pages at a sitting, but I had persevered, to be rewarded at last with a final segment so well written, so compelling, the author had me completely. He relentlessly accelerated his story. The villain had made just one slight misstep. Lady Smith .357 in hand, stilling her breathing, our protagonist waited in deep snow for the right moment. Her finger rested on the trigger, calm, ready.

Enveloped in the thriller's climax, I reached occasionally with my left hand for the Austrian goblet. Each time I replaced it without lifting my eyes from the page. Tension grew. The heroine drew her antagonist where she wanted him. This time the goblet's base landed partly on the travertine tile coaster and more than half on air. What should have been an upright still life listed slowly over the edge.

It was already too late the instant I let go. The wine glass angled beyond recovery over the edge of the coaster. *Oh no!* screamed in my mind, even before the wine spilled.

I swiped reflexively at the tipping glass, hoping to avert the inevitable. The edge of my hand struck the bowl of the goblet just as the first splash flew over its rim. The blow propelled the glass and its crimson contents toward the drapery behind the cream brocade loveseat next to my chair. Mortified, I watched the wine and the goblet fly away from each other. Each nanosecond was agony as gravity had its way: the glass exploded into crystal shards, and the dark pinot noir strewn en route lay like a blood-red Jackson Pollock across the absorbent cushions.

Like every accident, it was already over. I felt embarrassed, anxious, remorseful, angry, resigned, all at once—a joint result of the wine calamity and the spy thriller's climax. I couldn't undo the spill. I let my eyes be pulled back to the final paragraph.

She squeezed the trigger. Blood splattered across a snow bank. It was over.

I put the book down. Suspended where fiction and reality merge was the same pattern on the loveseat, in pinot.

SAFE WAY

A Short Story

Emilio's mornings often started well before dawn when he and his partner got their first calls from the Highway Patrol dispatcher. Some days it could be one emergency after another; on others, they'd just sit drinking coffee in the hospital snack bar. This morning Al swung by, picked Emilio up, and aimed the ambulance toward the interstate.

Nine long hours later, his shift over but still in uniform, Emilio headed over to Safeway for a few things his wife had asked him to buy. Diapers were at the top of the list. Being an EMT required professional detachment, an ability to deal efficiently and objectively with situations most people hope they never face. He liked his job and was good at it, but he was always happy to leave the drama—or the boredom—behind each afternoon and go home to Susan and their Allysa. A welcoming smile from his wife, or a *"Daddy! Daddy!"* from their twenty-month-old daughter, and the warmth that filled him melted the workday away.

The Safeway store supplied the kitchen of every home in Cedarburg. The next nearest supermarket was twenty-two miles away, so everyone in town went to Safeway a few times a week. Megan was a regular shopper, and she was on her way there for her almost daily stop.

A glowing newlywed, Megan had grown up in Cedarburg. She and Jim rented a two-bedroom apartment six blocks from the retail center. This afternoon she was bubbly happy about her dad's arrival the next morning. He'd be staying with them for a week. Megan looked forward to Dad's visits, and she was glad the two most important men in her life liked each other so well. She hummed along with Vince Gill as she turned her cute new sedan off Seventh Street into the Safeway lot. She needed just a couple items before going home to put in a load of laundry and start supper.

Two other Cedarburg kids cruised aimlessly on residential streets north of Seventh.

"No sweat," Eric assured his boyhood buddy, who was intently biting a fingernail in the passenger seat of Eric's unfinished '69 Impala. The car's body looked like crap—once red, now rusty, some panels just gray primer with patches of Bondo, and the interior was a mess. But that baby could fly.

Eric went on in his confident tone. "I've done it lotsa times, and it's cool. Easy."

Sheldon looked skeptically at Eric.

"This is your initiation, Shelly," Eric continued. "Do this right and there'll be bigger things."

They drove around familiar streets as Eric laid everything out, and Shelly was gradually infected with Eric's excitement about the plan. *Maybe it* will *be cool,* he thought. Grabbing some lady's purse in a parking lot sounded easy enough, and they'd have some beer money. More, if they were lucky.

"Okay," said Shelly, with more bravado in his voice than he felt.

Safeway was ahead on the left. Eric hung his arm out the window to signal; his turn lights didn't work.

On the edge of the Safeway lot, Steve sat in a window booth at Denny's. He lived near Cedarburg and frequented the Safeway like everybody else. From the worn, slick, black vinyl seat, Steve looked over parked cars toward the prominent red sign on the front of the big-box building, and took in the sharp light of the clear autumn day outside. He wasn't a fast-food guy, but once in a while some fries sure tasted good. He took the last bite of his second burger and swished a final fry through the ketchup.

Mmm, he thought. *Bad, but so good.*

He'd be seeing Carolyn that night and needed a little something special from the Safeway. He got up, slid his beige jacket over his green plaid shirt, paid his bill at the register, and started walking toward the store.

●　　●　　●

The parking lot asphalt was already giving back some of the warmth it had borrowed from the September sun, but Emilio couldn't feel it. He was lying on the dark, pebbly pavement, and didn't know why. Noises—traffic on Seventh Street, a small plane getting louder, then softer—seemed far away. A humming sound, like a thousand happy bees somewhere nearby, didn't make sense.

He was too cold to shiver. Everything seemed dreamlike. He wasn't in pain. He wasn't even afraid. But he couldn't lift his head. He tried. Emilio realized he didn't feel his body at all. All he knew was cold, and that he couldn't move.

He willed his eyes to open, but the darkness remained. His fingers wouldn't listen when he told them to wiggle. His hands may as well have been someone else's. Emilio noticed details like he would have with an accident victim, but this was himself. Even more befuddling was the way he was strangely unbothered by it all. By all rights he should have been going crazy with fear, but he had a pervasive assurance that things would be all right. They needed diapers for their little girl.

Emilio's memory had been flash-frozen. Oh, he knew his name, and Susan and Allysa, and all the usual and important stuff. He knew he'd pulled his F-150 into a space in the Safeway lot and gotten out. He had hit the lock button on his key fob and walked between parked cars toward the store entrance.

Sounds again, directionless, swirled around him. Soft, indistinct voices. He couldn't tell if they were coming from outside or in.

• • •

"Emilio Vasquez, Emergency Medical Technician, UMR Ambulance Service," Sergeant Phillips, Cedarburg County

Sheriff's Department, said, reading Emilio's badge aloud to no one in particular. "EMT."

Phillips spoke into his radio. "Apparent attempted robbery. A shooting. We have one deceased, two in custody, another in shock. Request medical assistance. Officers Blane and Gonzalez are interviewing the victim."

Numb and shaken, Megan was nevertheless able to answer most of the questions the officers gently put to her. They would piece together what had happened in the Safeway lot. At least three others saw the critical events just before the booming gunshots, but one of them wasn't talking and another couldn't. The third, a large, muscular young man in a green plaid shirt, a light jacket, and jeans, was talking animatedly with another officer.

• • •

Emilio remembered coming out of anesthesia when he'd had his tonsils out as a kid. His old country doctor had squeezed drops of ether onto a paper mask over eleven-year-old Emilio's face and told him if he didn't like the smell to just blow it away. Waking later was like floating slowly up from a deep well of black. That's how it was now. He couldn't see anything, but the enveloping darkness was starting to fade to charcoal gray.

• • •

Megan's right sleeve and most of the front of her light tan jacket were flecked with thick blood, drying in the slanting afternoon sunlight. She either didn't know or didn't care that her right cheek and side of her neck had also been splattered. Megan shifted her stare only between her hands and the officers questioning her, careful not to glance anywhere else. Covered with a dark blue blanket, the body lay where it had fallen, like a heavy sack of grain. Someone had brought a folding chair for Megan, and she gratefully sat. Officer Gonzalez draped another blue blanket around her shoulders.

"You opened your car door. Then what happened?" Officer Blane asked Megan. "Did you see the man coming?" The three were near the left front fender of Megan's white Subaru. Head down, she would have noticed her blood-flecked sleeve if her eyes had been focusing, but they weren't.

Closing them, Megan replied, "No. I opened the door just a little so I wouldn't bump the car next to mine, and squeezed out. When I turned to shut the door, he slammed me into it, grabbed my purse strap, and yanked. Hard. He pulled it off my arm so fast I couldn't do anything but yell."

A few yards away, a cop with a digital tablet asked the green-shirted man in the beige jacket his name. "Steve Jacobs," he replied. "Mortonson." His town was too small to have its own supermarket. The officer took his statement.

"I was walking across the lot from Denny's over there when that lady screamed. It was pure fear—went right through me. I didn't think; I just took off running toward where I thought she was."

Steve's loose clothes didn't disguise his athletic physique. And the officer, a pretty big guy himself, had to look up as he asked questions.

• • •

Emilio's attention was in a foggy dawn of faint but growing light. He still couldn't see anything, but he was coming out of it, slowly, slowly up out of the cold blackness.

• • •

When the witnesses' accounts were patchworked together, the story became whole. Shelly, the purse snatcher, had spun to sprint away from his victim, Megan, and had run between two cars, straight into Emilio, who was just a few feet away. He had looked up in response to Megan's chilling shriek and had seen Shelly rip the bag from her and take off. Already tensed, coiled, ready, he stopped the man with a straight-arm to the chest, and his full weight went behind the instinctive upper cut to Shelly's chin, decking him and apparently knocking him cold.

"Wow," was Emilio's reaction to what he'd just done, surprised and pleased the guy went down from one punch. He quickly squatted, pulled the purse from the unconscious man's hand, stood up, and turned toward the frozen Megan. With the start of a smile, Emilio looked at her eyes as he held the bag out to her. The grimace of abject terror on her face was confusing. The thought lightninged through his mind that maybe she mistook him for another robber. Then the world went impossibly bright white, then black—and Emilio lay on the asphalt.

Steve filled in the rest. As he sprinted across the pavement toward Megan he caught Emilio's confrontation with Shelly. A big rust-blotted Chevy blocked his way and he swerved around it. In his peripheral vision he saw a young man he'd later learn was Eric run around the other end of the Impala and point a long-barreled pistol at Emilio's back. The shot was very loud. Ears ringing, Steve was right on him, grabbing Eric's right arm and slamming it with adrenaline-fueled strength on the car's roof. The gun went off again, but Eric let it drop when pain seared his arm and involuntarily relaxed his hand. Eric was no match for Steve, who pinned him to the car and held him there.

Sirens. Flashing lights. People converging, crowding to see, then parting to let the police through.

Megan hadn't seen her assailant very well, but she'd remember the shooter's face, and the barrel of his gun, for the rest of her life. "He's the one you have over there," she said, nodding toward the police cruiser. Eric was in the back seat, cradling his broken arm with his left hand. An officer pressed the handcuffed Shelly firmly against the side of another squad car. Later Megan would remember Emilio's face, but it was too soon for that.

•   •   •

Emilio's fog was lifting. For the first time he had a gauzy vision of people, cars, commotion. He was there but he wasn't there. He saw his ambulance partner, Al, lift the edge of the blanket from a motionless form. A tranquil expanse of dark blood had spread from the fallen man's head and was seeping into the asphalt around it. Half his face had been blown off, exposing shattered bone and coagulating gore. Emilio recognized the other half as his own.

He wasn't cold anymore.

What's in a name?

—William Shakespeare

SHADES OF GRAY

"Are you the *real* John Gray?"

You'd be surprised how often I'm asked that by people wondering if I'm the more famous author. I always assure them I am real. I add that my wife is not from Venus; she's from Iowa.

I have the second most common first name and the sixty-ninth most common surname in America. An Internet search for "John Gray" turns up at least 76,000 results. Even Googling my whole name, John Clinton Gray, turns up matches. Wikipedia thinks the most famous one was born in 1843: a John Clinton Gray who served as a New York Court of Appeals judge from 1888 until 1913, when pneumonia got him.

I was named after both my grandfathers. Had I been born last week I might go by a trendier name, like Noah Mason Gray or Jacob Justin Gray, but to me, my more traditional monikers are just fine. I've worn them a long time, after all. They're well broken in, comfortable. *John* derives from a Hebrew root meaning "God is gracious," and *Clinton* refers to a "town on a hill" in Old English. It's amazing, but I actually live in a town on a hill, and if it weren't for the grace of God I know I wouldn't be here. So I think my prescient parents got my names just right.

Except, well...there are so many of us...

John Grays alive today include a television news anchor in Albany, New York; a mayor of Greenland, Arkansas; a Canadian ice hockey player; an English cricketer; and a fugitive from the law in Trinidad, Texas. In the Cayman Islands, there's a John Gray High School.

In addition to the judge, among dead John Grays are an English poet and priest; the first practitioner of homeopathy in the United States; an Aussie rules footballer; a U.S. Civil War Medal of Honor recipient; the founder of Gray's School of Art in Aberdeen, Scotland; and the first president of Ford Motor Company. There was also a chemistry professor at the U.S. Naval Academy—my grandfather.

Hey, it could be worse. The most common male name in America is James Smith. Search that, and up come 460,000 results. There's even a Jim Smith Society with annual conferences. So being one of 76,000 isn't *that* bad. After all, I am the real one.

That's why I love road trips, dude.
It's like doing something without actually doing anything.

— John Green, *An Abundance of Katherines*

WHEN PIGS FLEW

In Levittown, Long Island—Suburbia, USA—childhood lasted a long time. In the 1950s and '60s we didn't know we were baby boomers. The term first appeared in the *Washington Post* in 1970, and by then, most of us had flown our hometown.

As little kids, our outdoor adventures were confined to the near vicinity of our own homes, and we were always watched by our moms or neighbor-moms. Once we achieved school age, excursions were defined by how far we could walk, which wasn't far—seldom more than a few houses in any direction, except for going the three blocks to Wisdom Lane Elementary and back.

Of course, as we got older, explorations grew longer and grander. Tricycles extended our range a little, then clip-on, metal-wheeled roller skates a bit more. A more significant increase came with small bicycles with training wheels, and then, one magical day, *without* the training wheels. But an exponential expansion came when our legs had finally grown long enough for the two-wheelers of Phase II Adolescence—*real* bikes, with twenty-six-inch-diameter wheels and smooth direct-chain drives. Almost overnight, our range of freedom expanded from blocks to miles. From about age nine until driver's ed, bicycles were our primary transportation.

Then, a new world opened.

"Ah, memory lane stuff," stage-sighed Ellen.

Six of us were sitting around Ellen's kitchen table. Fifty years ago we grew up within three Levittown blocks of one another. Today we'd walked the old neighborhood and taken smartphone pictures of each other standing in front of the houses we grew up in. Though she hasn't always, Ellen lives in her original family home on Target Lane, where she hosted our reunion. In our much-younger years we all spent a lot of time in that kitchen; Ellen's parents were more understanding and open-minded than most.

A half-century condensed into *now* as we reminisced. Despite our obviously aging bodies, for minutes at a stretch we were teens again. Pauses briefly appeared when memories no one needed or wanted to talk about surfaced and then sank anew, but mostly the conversation skipped along at a bright pace. Along with Ellen, present were Karen and four guys: Dick, Doug, Bill, and me. Each one's stories unraveled piecemeal from old, tightly wound balls of used yarn. At times we'd realize we were pulling a common thread, and a nearly whole tale would emerge to recompose itself.

The topic came around to cars. In the sixties, just a few Levittown boys owned their own while still in high school. The luckiest of the rest of us got to ride in our friends' cars; the less fortunate were ferried by parents, still used bikes, or, once in a while, got to drive the family car.

The teenaged Billy, as we knew Bill then, harbored an ardent desire to have his own automobile. It burned in him like a Heliarc welding torch. When he was at last old enough, he came out as an entrepreneurial car buyer. I don't use *entrepreneur* to suggest Billy saw opportunities others didn't, though that's not inaccurate. He was the kind of entrepreneur who initiates an enterprise and accepts the inherent risks, foreseen or not. Billy seemed to consider just two criteria in his car buying: "Does it run?" and "Can I afford it?"—not necessarily in that order. Everything else was a risk he accepted.

Billy and another friend, Lee, were the first guys in our crowd to get their own wheels. Both were Fords, Lee's a home-painted, light blue, 1954 Customline straight-six sedan he and his brother, Jan, rebuilt from a scrap heap. Billy's was a baby-blue-and-rust '56 Ford Victoria two-door hardtop, a former police car he bought as-is at auction in 1963 for $65. It had a spotlight attached near the driver's side mirror, and a blue flashing light where the grill once was, operated by a switch on the dash. Its V-8 had a lot of hard miles on it, but the odometer didn't work so he never knew how many. The Vic was missing its Ford emblem and chrome airplane-like hood ornament, and the absence of a grill gave the car a toothless maw. None of these flaws made any difference to Billy; he did just enough on the car to keep it running.

Lee was really into his car; his '54 Ford became a work of reconditioned art. Billy was into what he could *do* with a car. Big difference. Lee basked in the pride of accomplishment. Billy loved the freedom it gave him. Some of Billy's friends loved the freedom it gave *them*, too.

A few of those, the males now sparser of hair and wider of paunch, sat with him now in Ellen's kitchen. From the loosely linked subconscious minds of three of them, out spun a true yarn of four guys and a pig.

Before you start imagining things, "the Pig" was Billy's car. Whether his '56 Victoria was so nicknamed because of its appearance, its condition, the noises it made, fumes it emitted, gasoline it consumed, or some combination of the five, it was the Pig. Actually, it was *Pig II*. Pig I was a big old early-fifties dark green Plymouth Billy's father had given him before he could even legally drive. Billy had run the bald tires right off Pig I by the time Pig II came along.

The four guys in the tale were Billy, Doug, Dick, and Carpino. Not me.

I don't know why we always called Carpino by his surname, but we did. Tommy Carpino took after his Sicilian father with his short, unruly dark hair and charcoal eyes. At seventeen he was gangly and goofy-looking with jug-handle ears that stuck straight out. Carpino was smart at school, but with his friends he was a comedian, with goofy jokes and goofy antics to match his looks. His friend Ritchie taught him car mechanic skills, and there wasn't anything with a motor Carpino couldn't fix.

Billy was the fairest of the foursome, with boy-next-door good looks. His blue eyes, ready smile, and Ricky Nelson brown hair made girls look at him twice. Had Billy possessed *half* Carpino's outgoing easiness, he could have had his pick of the prettiest. Billy, the entrepreneurial risk-taker, was reticent only around girls.

Dick was a school year younger than Billy. He dressed in denim, a folk follower of early Dylan and contemporaries. He was observant, a serious thinker. His liberal ideals were already well-rooted. He tried to hide his forehead zits with a mop of dark brown hair that flopped over his right eye. Dick's wry, dry wit often went over the others' heads, despite his being the shortest of the four.

Doug dressed like a wannabe greaser, with a pack of cigarettes rolled in his white Hanes T-shirt sleeve, the rest of his uniform being black chino pants, black shoes with heel taps, black socks, slicked-back black hair, and a sneer. He had a mean streak that came out once in a while, and odoriferous feet. Doug seldom smiled, except at his own jokes, but the others knew he was a good guy.

All four smoked. Marlboros, mostly. A carton cost $2.50 at the A&P then, and some check-out clerks would look the other way if the buyer seemed young.

Billy, Dick, Doug, and Carpino were always looking for something cool to do, urges born of universal teen ennui.

Dick initiated the idea of a road trip to his Uncle Bill's in Connecticut. The eccentric uncle lived in Storrs, a place Dick had loved visiting often in earlier boyhood. It didn't take coercion to get Billy, Carpino, and Doug enthused about getting out of Levittown for a weekend. Of course they couldn't just take off in Pig II without arrangements and permission, but Dick made the former and each got the latter.

My parents were not lenient. It was preordained they'd never let me go on an excursion like this with a bunch of buddies. Not to Connecticut. Not to anywhere. Not with those guys. And not, certainly, in Billy's car. Dick knew enough to not even ask.

For the four, getting away from home for a couple days was reason enough to make the trip. Was it part of their coming of age? J.D. Salinger's *The Catcher in the Rye* was already a classic, but to attribute Holden Caulfield-esque qualities to their Connecticut adventure would be a complication both unnecessary and untrue. They were just four Levittown guys with a car, tired of cruising Hempstead Turnpike looking for chicks. Not that that ever worked, anyway. Not in Pig II.

It was easy to agree to head to Dick's Uncle Bill's because (a) it's only 166 miles and less than four hours from Levittown, as the Pig flies; (b) it was a new adventure; and (c) it was a free place to stay. They all had a little money from their summer jobs—enough to chip in for gas, not starve, and to create an illusion of independence for a weekend.

It was July 1964. What a summer... JFK's assassination remained raw in American hearts. President Johnson signed the Civil Rights Act into law. Race riots in Pennsylvania and New Jersey, civil war in the Congo, nuclear arms tests by the US, USSR, and UK, and the start of the US bombing of Vietnam, all smeared across the TV news. The New York World's Fair opened that spring and summer, and everybody went to Flushing Meadows, Queens, maybe more than once. The Fair was inspiring, futuristic, and fascinating; also costly and crowded. The Beatles embarked on their second US tour and the Rolling Stones their first, their songs vying with one another at or near the top of the radio pop charts.

On a Friday afternoon, the four sixteen- and seventeen-year-olds set out westward in Pig II across the wilds of Nassau County into Queens. WABC's Dan Ingram announced the Rolling Stones' hit single "It's All Over Now," and Billy, at the wheel, turned the volume up. The toll to cross the then-new Throgs Neck Bridge to the Bronx was seventy-five cents, but the boys were feeling pretty rich, and the bridge brought their destination closer. Jan & Dean harmonized "Surf City." In his hyped DJ voice, Ingram set up "A Hard Day's Night," the Beatles' latest. The sun was high in the south, all of Pig II's windows were rolled down, and the guys were smokin' and rockin' to the radio. Life was good.

Mostly good, anyway. The hot July afternoon was the *second* reason Pig II's windows were open as far as they could go. The first was the exhaust fumes pouring intermittently through the defroster vents. Pig II processed its engine exhaust through the passenger cabin whenever it felt like it, prompting driver and passengers to stub out their cigarettes and to hang this or that extremity out the windows as if they were lungs.

Billy punched his pre-set radio button to 1010 WINS during a WABC commercial. Loudly and poorly, all four sang along to the inspired lyrics of Manfred Mann's "Doo Wah Diddy Diddy." The "dum diddy doo" part struck Carpino so funny he laughed 'til he started coughing.

After the bridge crossing, signs led our explorers to the Thomas E. Dewey Thruway and the ramp onto Hutchinson River Parkway. The Supremes sang them through New Rochelle, but it took only the first notes of the Dixie Cups' "Chapel of Love" to compel Billy to punch Pig II's tuner back to WABC.

A friendly "Welcome to Connecticut" sign greeted them. Then Greenwich, Norwalk, Bridgeport, and on; more Beatles, Stones, Four Seasons, Martha & The Vandellas, Four Tops, Dionne Warwick, the Drifters...

It was Dick who was doing most of the remembering around Ellen's table. Except for details about cars, Billy's comments ranged from "Oh, that's right" to "Dick, how do you remember all this?" Doug's standard contributions were "I don't remember" or "Was I drunk?" But collective memories were stirred, and yard by yard the story spun out.

As they skirted New Haven on the Wilbur Cross Parkway, heading northward, the Beatles' "Love Me Do" faded in and out until static overcame it. Billy twisted Pig II's tuner knob and happened upon "Big D" WDRC, Hartford. The final refrain of "Hello Dolly" in Louis Armstrong's sandpaper baritone filled the car. The guys put up with lesser songs until the Beatles, Stones, or Beach Boys came around again. Whenever number one "I Get Around" came on, Carpino would lunge from the back seat to turn the volume up to just short of distorting. It was the consummate road song.

Carpino parodied it, referring to the main drag in Levittown: "I got bugged driving up and down the old Turnpike. Now my buddies and me are takin' a hike... I get around, round, round, I get around." The other three yelled, "Shut up!" in unison.

Nearing Hartford, they slowed on the Berlin Turnpike to Peter and Gordon's "A World Without Love." Billy worried Pig II might overheat, but it behaved itself, except, of course, for the suffocating exhaust through the defroster vents.

Onward they slogged through Hartford, and headed east to Mansfield—the last leg. Jan & Dean's "Dead Man's Curve" didn't make Billy lighten his foot on the gas. Pig II's sporadic asphyxiation attempts notwithstanding, the quartet made it to Dick's Uncle Bill's place in Storrs in late afternoon.

"Wild Willy," as Dick's mother's sister's black-sheep husband was referred to by friend and foe, was a shortish, muscular, stocky, whiskey-sipping janitor and former nurse. Bell's palsy had left half his face slack, and his words emerged from the side of his mouth. Many assumed it was deliberate; it did give him a mildly sinister look. But the "wild" moniker derived from his oddball penchant for saying and doing outrageously unexpected things. Dick's Uncle Bill *lived* out in left field.

Even I knew this, firsthand. He once goosed me on the stairs in Dick's Levittown house as we were going up to Dick's room in our preteen summer uniforms of shorts and T-shirt—Dick first, I close behind, and Wild Willy behind me. My rear guard was down, and I yelped and sprang three steps at once. My shock was threefold: First, that he really did it; goosing was something boys might do, but not a grown-up. Second, the rigidity of his finger. Third, his unerring aim. Decades later I learned both Carpino and Billy were on the receiving end of Wild Willy's intrusions during their Pig II visit. Over time, all our digital memories soured from semifunny to off-beat to weird.

So the boys arrived in Storrs that sunny July afternoon. The point had been to get there, and there they were. The other three looked to Dick for what to do the next day. Saturday was to be their one perfect day of freedom.

Storrs, Connecticut, is the site of UCONN, the University of Connecticut. Billy wanted to drive near campus to girl-watch, and since he was driver and Pig owner, that's what they did first on Saturday morning. It was a disappointment. No classes on summer weekends. No co-eds in miniskirts.

They spent the rest of the day bombing around Tolland and Windham Counties, hitting places Dick knew. They hung out, smoked, listened to the radio, and each in his own way savored the imminence of adulthood, imagining it much closer than it really was.

Dick directed Billy to Lake Wangumbaug, near Coventry, home of Revolutionary War patriot Nathan Hale. The countryside had that hazy green, shimmering, summery look about it, and the humid heat invited them to swim. Dick, Doug, Billy, and Carpino donned their nylon suits and headed for the coolness.

Then the boys were back on the road again, refreshed, enveloped in Connecticut's verdant summer luxuriance. Pig II nonchalantly gave the four another carbon monoxide bath. Dick, Doug, and Carpino stuck their heads out their windows, and Billy drove on, heading southeast through Willimantic and on to Windham on the road to Scotland. Doug announced Scotland was farther than he wanted to go, but he was the only one who chuckled.

They took Route 203 toward South Windham with Getz & Gilberto's "The Girl from Ipanema" smoothing the way. Cruising the rural road, they took a railroad crossing too fast. Pig II bottomed hard, then lurched. Billy braked it to a stop. Maybe it was a cosmic joke when Roy Orbison's voice lamented "It's Over" on Big D, Hartford, right then.

After inspection, Carpino pronounced a broken rear axle. Inexplicable to the other three, he also said they could drive on it.

It wasn't far back to Storrs, and they made it, slowly, without further drama. Nobody spoke much. Even Beatles and Beach Boys favorites on the radio didn't help lift the pall, and Roger Miller's twangy "Dang Me" evoked no smiles. Pig II, probably annoyed at the way it had been treated, pumped noxious fumes into the cabin the whole way.

Sunday morning began with an argument among the boys. Carpino and Billy were cocksure Pig II could make it back to Levittown, subluxated axle and all. Dick and Doug wanted nothing to do with it.

Wild Willy joined the fray. "You're nuts to drive that heap."

Carpino came back, "Bullshit! We'll make it, no sweat.

"Yeah, when pigs fly," muttered Uncle Bill.

Dick and Doug decided they'd had enough and set out to hitchhike back to Long Island. Billy and Carpino drove the injured car. All four got home without incident.

That was the last of Pig II, though. Within days, Billy's affections turned to a very used gray '55 Plymouth: Pig III.

Pig III saw only local Long Island adventures during its brief stint as Billy's favorite. "At least it's not trying to gas us" was the best the guys could say about it. But since they were nearly dead when he bought them, Billy's cars never lasted long. One day a yellow four-door 1956 Oldsmobile Rocket 88 convertible was parked in the street in front of Billy's house on Shotgun Lane. Like its predecessors, Pig IV's better days were long past. It was missing a fair amount of paint and a rear passenger window, but its rumbly V-8 still had plenty of power. The big boat—almost eighteen feet long—was fun to drive. Carpino and Doug thought so too. Now and then they'd hot-wire it and go on a joyride while the more diligent Billy was in high school class. Porcine purloining was a favorite sport until the last time, when Billy saw the two roar by the school in his Olds.

In Ellen's Levitt house kitchen, the unwound tales of boyhood, Pigs, and Connecticut lay exposed on the table. I don't think I was the only one smelling a waft of exhaust fumes in the temporary silence. We'd all just time-traveled, and were back.

When young people are in a hurry to get out on their own, make decisions, do important things, the innocence of the time is easily overlooked in the rush to grow up. A year after their once-ever Pig II weekend in Connecticut, Carpino and Billy were in the US Navy, and months later, Doug enlisted in the Air Force and was sent to Vietnam. Dick was drafted by the Army but had a deferment. Doug and Dick had each met the loves of their lives by this point, the women they're with today. We learned Carpino died a few years ago.

Bill still has a boyishness about him. He's owned other old cars, but that big yellow Olds was the last of the Pigs.

THE GIFT

A Short Story

When Emily invited Rob to move into her Studio City bunga-low they'd been a couple for almost a year. Neither of them liked hasty choices; they took their time, making sure. A year is a long time when you're twenty-six. In the months after Rob moved his stuff in, they often celebrated their merger several times a day.

Their girl-meets-boy thing had happened in a coffee shop near the university where Emily was working on her mas-ter's. Rob taught algebra and geometry at Everett Mason Middle School a mile away. They met while simultaneously reaching for the powdered chocolate shaker, touching fin-gertips before they'd ever seen each other's face. A year later they had no *if* question about getting married; only *when*.

Rob was a math teacher, but to Emily his long, slim body reminded her of an Olympic swimmer's. His lake-blue eyes always shone happily, and they danced when he smiled. Emily was the same cute, petite girl she'd blossomed into as a teenager, but now she carried herself with a woman's assurance. She wore her dark hair shoulder length, often pulled back. Her striking eyes were a cinnamon-green, like her mother's—and her uncle's.

When Emily's uncle Jack began traveling more and living overseas, he invited her to live rent-free in the Studio City home he'd bought back when even a wannabe screenwriter could buy one. After Jack was lost in a climbing accident in Nepal, Emily learned he'd left the fully furnished house to her. She could never have afforded it on her own; just the property taxes and regular bills were a challenge. New furniture would have to wait.

As a girl Emily had been close to Uncle Jack, but with her starting college and his traveling all the time, she hadn't seen him nearly as much. There were emails, of course, and photos from wonderful places. Surprise gifts would arrive now and then. But other than through family stories, some of them more supposition than fact, she had hardly known her mother's adventurous, black sheep brother once she was older and on her own. According to family lore he'd written screenplays for two blockbuster films in the same year back in the 1970s, and he'd made successful real estate investments. To Emily, he was simply her enigmatic Uncle Jack, and she thanked him every month for the mortgage payment she didn't have.

Emily could feel Uncle Jack's presence in the house where he'd lived for so many years. She told Rob about it.

"It's not a haunted house kind of feeling," she said. "Nothing scary. It's more like he's just around, watching over me."

Her thoughts drifted on an internal breeze, resisting being forced into words. "I don't feel him all the time," she added, "but when I do it's always an 'everything's okay' feeling."

Lifting those wonderful eyes to him, she asked, "Rob, am I weird?"

Rob smiled, drew Emily into his arms, and gently kissed her for lingering seconds.

"No. Not weird. Beautiful. Smart. Creative," he said, kissing her between each word. "Definitely not weird."

Emily's mother had told her at the memorial service that Jack had been lead climber when a critical piton worked loose and he plunged into an ice crevasse as large as a canyon. A fellow climber described watching, horrified, as Jack at first floated in the subzero air like a free-base jumper, then blurred past blue-white walls to disappear into the black below. "He didn't make a sound," his friend had said.

"He loved you, you know," Emily's mother said to her, breaking the silence, her moist eyes punctuating the sentence. Looking away at nothing, she added, "I always felt he was a little jealous of me for having you."

• • •

The dream first came to Emily early that summer. It wasn't an odd or disquieting dream, and she'd dismissed it. When it recurred a week later, though, repeating itself with a couple new memorable details, the experience began climbing her top-forty chart of strange things. She couldn't remember ever having the same dream twice. Then it came a third time, and a fourth. In the following weeks it returned again and again, playing out almost identically as often as two nights out of three. She told Rob about it so many times all she had to say now was, "Had it again."

She talked to her sister in Michigan, who agreed with Emily that a recurring dream was indeed a bit bizarre. "Em, if you tell me the dream once more I'm afraid I'll start having it too." Her kidding did nothing to assuage Emily's seeping unease. Rob was understanding and caring but had no answers. Each time the dream came she wanted more than ever to know what was going on. Searching the Web for dream symbolism didn't get her anywhere.

It wasn't frightening; most of the dream was grandly beautiful. The sight of the massive blue-white glacier calving into the sea was breathtakingly exquisite. She seldom viewed it as you would from a cruise ship hugging the Alaskan coast. Sometimes she was high above an icy, petulant sea, with an eagle's vision. She could be underwater, watching the massive, falling berg from below, as an orca or humpback might. At other times she was in a kayak far below the glacial edge, looking up at the massive ice cliff from water level. But no matter her vantage point, in the dream Emily always heard a deep, subwooferish groan just before the ice let go with an explosive *crack!* It was her personal National Geographic program. She said it was just weird seeing it over and over.

After athletic lovemaking one night, they slept. Later Rob stirred slightly and reached to draw Emily closer, but didn't feel her beside him. He awoke enough to listen for her in the bathroom, but heard nothing except the sounds the house always made. A car passing on the street outside touched the edge of his attention, its tires' muffled grind on asphalt sounding almost like gentle surf. He opened his eyes, now certain Emily wasn't there. No lights were on in the house, no silvery-white glow from the monitor in their tiny office across the hall. Rob shed the sheet from his legs and got up.

He padded the few steps from bedroom to kitchen and found Emily standing there, motionless. She did not hear him approach. She stood, naked, relaxed, still. Amber luminescence from the sodium streetlight filtered through the oleanders near the kitchen window, its warm light quivering on the soft curves of her body. Rob paused behind her, enchanted by the living sculpture. Only the refrigerator pulsed and hummed, its compressor pumping refrigerant through its veins.

"Emily?" Rob whispered. "You okay?" He stepped softly around her to see her face. "Emily?"

Her eyes were open, but empty. Emily was staring, her gaze vacant. "Emily?" Rob repeated, softly. Then, "Emily?" a bit louder. She neither heard nor saw him.

She's asleep, he realized. He'd heard of sleepwalking, of course, but had no firsthand experience of it.

"Emily? Let's go back to bed, okay?"

He touched her shoulder with his fingertips. She trembled a little, then yielded to his guidance. They shuffled together down the hall to bed. Emily lay on her side and pulled the sheet up. Rob slid in behind her, spooning his body with hers. He looped his arm over her to hold her close, his hand softly cupping her breast, one of so many ways they fit just right together. She sighed and stirred a little. "Emily?" Rob whispered.

"Mm-hmm," she murmured as she turned toward him.

"Awake?" Rob whispered. She answered him with a full, warm kiss. He wondered, but just briefly, if sleepwalking was a serious thing.

"Had it again," she called from the shower in the morning. Rob stepped in and joined her. She turned into his wet, slippery embrace as he answered, "I know."

Toweling each other off, Rob told her about finding her standing in the kitchen, asleep, and leading her back to bed. "I don't remember any of that," Emily mused. Flashing a smile, she added, "I remember other good stuff, though," and kissed him quickly before turning toward her closet.

Alone later, Emily Googled *somnambulism*. She skimmed enough to learn it usually doesn't indicate a serious health issue; that awakening a sleepwalker in the act poses little or no danger; and that medical science can't explain the phenomenon. That's all good to know, she thought, but still it bothered her more than she'd admit to Rob.

Over dinner that night the couple agreed that if Emily sleepwalked again and Rob woke up as he had the previous night, he'd gently wake her, mid-walk. Maybe they'd find out how the dream and the sleepwalking were connected.

No calving icebergs visited Emily that night or the next, but on the third the dream returned. This time she viewed the glacier set aglow by angled afternoon sunlight. She swooped down to skim the whitecaps at its base. Emily was unaware of getting out of bed.

Rob stirred, arose, and followed her slow, careful steps into the kitchen. Immersed in the dream, Emily heard the deep groan of grinding ice as the towering berg cracked free above her, sliding and crashing into the cold black water. For Rob, the only audible sound in the kitchen was the side-by-side fridge, and all he could see was his beautiful Emily standing in front of it.

"Emily? Emily!" he repeated more urgently when she didn't respond. He stepped toward her and embraced her from behind, holding her in case he startled her. *"Emily!"*

"Rob?" she said, in a child's small voice. And after a pause, "Had it again..."

Sleepily she mumbled, "Uncle Jack took my hand and drew me down the hall..."

She looked around, awakening fully.

"We're in the kitchen!" she announced.

Over the ensuing nights, Rob awakened the sleepwalking Emily three more times, always in the kitchen. Each time she described her experience the same way. The lead-up could be longer or shorter, and the viewing perspective varied, but Uncle Jack always led her, and the dream always ended with the crashing fall of ice into the sea. They regarded the whole dreaming/sleepwalking thing as a puzzle, a mystery, a game. After Emily awoke in the kitchen each time, they'd return to bed where their hands and mouths would reignite each other. They'd join until their urgency crested, then melt into sweet sleep.

In their morning shower Rob asked Emily how she knew it was her uncle Jack. "Do you see him?" he wondered aloud.

Emily replied, eyes closed while she shampooed, "No. I don't see him. He's just there." She and Rob rotated carefully in the tight shower stall so she could rinse her hair. "It's the same feeling I used to have when I was a little girl and I'd sit on his lap. He always gave me his full attention, and I felt like I was the only one in the world who mattered."

With both hands she slicked her hair back, then wiped water from her face just as Rob's mouth covered hers in a wet kiss.

"Sometimes when I really notice my eyes in the mirror," Emily went on after the pleasant interruption, "I see Uncle Jack's and my mom's, too. My uncle called us the 'Cinnamon-green Club.' He said we were the only three members in the whole world."

From the start Rob had been enchanted by Emily's extraordinary hazel eyes with their constellations of reddish, golden flecks. He'd seen her mother's, but he hadn't known Emily's uncle shared the rarity.

● ● ●

On the next sleepwalking occasion, Rob's impulse was to awaken the standing Emily sooner, just to see if something would be different. It was.

"What was that?" Emily said, stirring from her standing sleep.

"What was what?"

"That sound."

Rob thought a moment. The only sound in the kitchen was the refrigerator doing its thing. "I think it was the ice-maker," he replied. "I didn't hear anything else."

"That's the sound," said Emily, excitement growing in her voice. "That's the sound the iceberg makes!"

Indeed, the icemaker sounded like an advancing miniature glacier, groaning and crackling, then noisily calving ice cubes into the plastic bin in the freezer. But it seemed far-fetched that the icemaker could be the cause of the dream.

As an experiment, Rob turned the device off. For the next week, with the icemaker disabled, Emily didn't dream of the calving glacier, and didn't sleepwalk. They turned the icemaker back on to see what would happen. On the second night the dream returned and Emily again stood before the refrigerator, asleep.

She related the whole story to a psych professor at her university, and he ventured his opinion that the sounds from the icemaker were stimulating Emily's subconscious. "No icemaker, no dream," he concluded. She didn't tell him about Uncle Jack's presence.

Emily and Rob had figured out the icemaker-dream connection on their own. A part of the puzzle was solved, but their nagging *"why?"* remained. But they left the icemaker off and their lives went happily on.

•   •   •

Rob got home from school on a hot afternoon and opened the freezer to pull out one of the ice cube trays they'd been using since killing the icemaker. *That thing just takes up space,* he thought, looking at the mechanism in the freezer. He left and came back with a Phillips screwdriver, and began removing the icemaker's mounting plate from the rear wall of the freezer. As he backed the last screw out, the hefty mechanism came loose in his hand. Taped behind it was a frosty plastic envelope. Hand-printed block letters on it read "EMILY."

Rob was still staring at the kitchen counter when Emily breezed in, dropped her backpack on a chair by the door, and hugged him around the waist. It took only a few hours apart for them to miss each other, and even afternoon reunions often led to bed.

"Hi," Emily said huskily. Rob smiled back after their protracted kiss.

"Look at this," he exhaled, nodding toward the envelope on the counter behind him. He told her quickly about finding it taped to the freezer wall behind the icemaker. Emily read her name and picked up the thin but unexpectedly weighty parcel.

"Behind the *icemaker*...?" she began. The rest of her thought slipped away like dandelion seeds in a breeze. "Uncle Jack..."

Emily took a pair of scissors from a drawer, cut the envelope, and slid the contents out. Five coins, each in its own small plastic sleeve, lay on the counter: two gold and three silver. They were old. The earliest date Emily and Rob could read through the hoary plastic was 1797. In another sleeve was a folded paper. Emily slit the plastic and opened the small note.

"Dear Emily, I want you to have these. Have a wonderful life, sweet girl. To me, you are the daughter I never had. All my love, Uncle Jack."

Emily's eyes brimmed. Tears crested her lids and spilled down her cheeks. She let them run, staring at the paper she held in both hands.

Uncle Jack intended these for me all along... Her thoughts raced. *But...the refrigerator?*

As if being jarred awake, she suddenly understood. *The freezer was just a hiding place. Uncle Jack didn't plan to die in Nepal.*

"Rob," she said, "Uncle Jack found a way back to tell us..."

The note mattered as much to Emily as the gifts. She felt enfolded in love. "I had no idea," she whispered, looking at Rob and then back at the frozen treasures. "No idea."

Rob held her. A mélange of sadness and joy rippled softly through Emily, then stilled to gratitude. She wiped her eyes.

Checking the coins out online brought more surprises. "This 1804 coin could be worth a lot," Emily said, as they both read the screen. On it was a photo that looked just like the silver dollar in her hand.

Over dinner they enjoyed imagining what they'd do if the coins were indeed valuable—take sabbaticals, replace their 2004 Toyota, travel, buy new furniture, pay off student loans, get the roof fixed... "Let's not go too far," Rob cautioned after a while. "We need to find out just what your uncle Jack gave you."

They spent two days researching firms specializing in numismatic appraisals, checked references, and chose one in downtown L.A. Three weeks later Emily and Rob sat opposite Mr. Reeves in the offices of Humboldt, Smith & O'Neill. Their five coins were arrayed on a black velvet tray on the lustrous rosewood table between them. A security guard stood by the door.

Reeves spoke in a reverent tone. "I am pleased to assure you that you possess five extremely rare and valuable coins." He went on, "Their authenticity and provenance have been certified and their value independently appraised by three of the best experts in the country. The 1861 Coronet twenty dollar gold piece may be the finest example of the coin known to exist. We have a buyer eager for the 1804 U.S. silver dollar, should you wish to sell. It is a most desirable U.S. coin to a collector. *Very* desirable—conservatively valued, this one alone is worth about four million dollars. At auction, probably more."

"Wow," choked Emily, barely able to get the word out. *"Wow!"*

Rob exhaled slowly. They looked at each other. Neither could possibly smile more broadly. Only Mr. Reeves's solemn presence restrained the nouveau millionairess from jumping and shrieking. The elevator's security camera was the sole witness as she and Rob hugged and hopped and shouted and laughed all the way down, then went home to celebrate.

It took about a month to arrange all they needed to. Rob was granted his sabbatical, Emily dropped her fall classes, and two days after the wedding the couple were off to Kathmandu, first stop on their around-the-world honeymoon. Emily and Rob were going to the Himalayas, but not to climb. They had to see *Kangchenjunga*, third tallest mountain in the world, for themselves. High on its southwestern face was Uncle Jack's ice-bound tomb.

The cloud-shrouded mountain's imposing presence filled Emily. Sensings of serenity, finality, eternity, wafted in soft waves through her heart.

"I feel him, Rob," she exhaled. "Uncle Jack is here."

Rob and Emily stood, holding mittened hands. They didn't need to talk. She wept openly when their guide told her the translation of the mountain's name: "Five Treasures of Snows."

WORLD'S END

There's an art to skipping stones, but it's not hard. Grip a thin, flat-ish stone between thumb and forefinger and fling it hard, sidearm, parallel to and just above the water's surface. When the flat faces of stone and water meet just right, the rock planes satisfyingly, skipping a dozen times or more before losing speed and disappearing into the deep. As a kid, I could content myself for hours skipping stones, watching their serial rippled wakes form and disperse.

Oceans are challenging, but just about any reasonably still pond, stream, or lake is suitable for rock skipping. Of course, you need a good supply of the right kind of stones. When I was a kid, I found the mother lode in a state park in north-central Pennsylvania.

Dad discovered World's End State Park in a Triple-A guidebook, and after our first family camping trip there it became an annual summer tradition. I must have been seven the first time because Dad drove our new maroon 1954 Plymouth station wagon there, stuffed with gear and the five of us. We camped in our two green canvas tents, sap-stained tarpaulins rigged between pine trees and pulled taut over Mom's rustic outdoor kitchen and conjoined campground tables. The last item to be set up was a cloth hammock strung between pines. I always found it tippy, but I can see my father napping there, a Leon Uris novel spread words-down on his chest.

We loved the place. We went camping once or twice every summer, and World's End was our family favorite. The drive from our home on Long Island was about 220 miles, and it felt interminable. We kids could answer our own *are we there yet?* when we finally spied the Forksville General Store and covered bridge a mile and a half from the park's entrance. We'd stop and Dad would buy a block of ice and Mom a few days' perishable basics. If we pleaded successfully, my sister, brother, and I would get ice cream sandwiches or fudgesicles.

When I was little I wasn't much help setting up camp except to hold tent poles while Dad did the rest. As soon as I was free to run off, I was at the creek, skipping rocks.

We siblings became adept at finding pine knots in fallen, well-rotted trees in the woods. Once dried, the resinous knots burned long and hot in our never-out campfires, and supplemented the pine bark firewood brought in from a local sawmill by the park rangers. Acrid smoke wafted constantly and sometimes stung our eyes, but the predominant smell of World's End was fresh pine. The air sang with it.

Dad would sometimes broil steaks or burgers or hot dogs over campfire coals or Kingsford charcoal, and Mom cooked things on a Coleman stove pretty much like she did on her electric range at home. Camping trips weren't much of a vacation for her. She did find an easy meal we all liked, though, and Dinty Moore Beef Stew in its red, blue, and white cans became regular camp fare. Better known for its ubiquitous Spam, the Hormel Company still makes Dinty Moore. Outdoors, eating from aluminum plates set on red-and-white-checked oilcloth, we couldn't get enough of the salty mixture of small beef chunks, cooked-to-death carrot wheels, and potato cubes in a tomatoey gravy. Mom tried a few times to feed us Dinty Moore Stew at home, but it didn't go over well. We loved it camping, but back in Levittown it was yucky.

We hiked, fished a little, jumped into the icy water of the creek's swimming hole, and went on occasional outings to nearby geologic features Dad had read about and wanted to see. Generally, though, we lazed around at World's End. Of course my preferred avocation was skipping rocks. Did you know a team of French physicists ascertained that an angle of about twenty degrees between the stone and the water's surface is optimal? And according to the *Guinness Book,* the world record is fifty-one skips? I never made twenty, but I'd throw until my arm tired, and come back to fling more.

Visiting World's End annually, we developed enjoyable routines. Driving to see black bears forage in a local dump was an occasional family event, but by year three we had a unanimously favorite summer-evening pastime: Following dinner, after the last aluminum plate had been sterilized in boiling water, dried, and stored, like everything else, in raccoon-proof, latched boxes, we'd pile into the blue-and-white '56 Ford wagon for a drive up the mountain road to Loyalsock Canyon Vista, a sunset overlook. The soft wooded mounds of the Appalachians spread before us like enormous green ocean swells, all the way to the hazy horizon. On the intentionally slow drive back to camp we'd count how many deer we could spot before dusk turned to dark. One year Dad surprised us by having a powerful spotlight plugged into the cigarette lighter and clamped on the rearview mirror arm, and our deer-watching time extended into night. The best thing about these camping trips, really, was having Dad full-time for a week.

The summer just after I turned thirteen, when we were camping in the World's End pines again, I met a girl at the creek.

She was blonde, pretty, and each morning for several in a row she was sitting alone on a rock at water's edge when I got there. She always wore jeans, and each day a different top—a tee or a sweatshirt, depending on the early morning's temperature. The centerpiece of the campgrounds, Loyalsock Creek, hurries through its rounded mountain ravine, and the sun doesn't reach in to directly warm its rocky banks until almost eight on summer days. I saw her in the softer light of new morning.

The first time we spoke I'd been skipping rocks across the creek when another flat stone zipped expertly over the water in a path very near mine. She'd thrown it.

"Hi," she said, when I wheeled to see the stone's origin.

I'd expected to see my little brother, but there on the rock-strewn creek beach stood the cutest girl I'd seen since Karen, the cast member of TV's original *Mickey Mouse Club*. Of course I'd only known Karen in black and white, and this real girl was in 3-D and full color. She didn't offer her name, nor I mine, but that began our morning meetings. She and her family were camping at World's End too. Like us, they'd be there a week, and this was day two.

For all but one of the next five mornings she was at the creek first. Sometimes we'd throw rocks, or pick our ways over the larger ones that formed the creek's banks and bed. We'd sit and watch the water rush noisily, and sometimes talk a little in preadolescent awkwardness. Mostly we just liked being in close variable orbits about each other, talking seldom, touching never. Had I introduced her, my mom might have thought her a tomboy, but I didn't see her that way.

Afternoons she'd be with her family at the swimming hole most campers were drawn to when the days grew hot. I thought she was a knockout in her one-piece swimsuit, but I found her more alluring in jeans, because that's what she wore in the mornings when Loyalsock Creek was all ours.

Late in the week I caught her flailing arm to steady her while clambering over rocks. She probably wouldn't have fallen and didn't need rescuing, but she let me anyway. I learned her family would be leaving the next day.

That last morning, when I got to the creek, she wasn't there. I was so disappointed I ached. My eyes searched the visible stretch of creek, but no Jean Girl.

I skipped rocks, throwing them as hard as I could, when she came up behind me, just like the first morning.

"We're leaving today," she said.

"I know."

I also knew this was a permanent goodbye. She lived in Indiana or Illinois or somewhere out there, and my home was a few miles from the Atlantic. The moment glowed, golden. An energy tingled between us, a force that had grown daily and compelled me out of my sleeping bag and back to the creek every morning. I hadn't felt it this strongly before.

She straddled two rocks at the creek's edge, stood close, and smiled her freckled Karen smile. Her shining blue eyes danced on my face. The hairs on my arms rose. She shifted even closer, our faces and bodies nearer than they'd ever been, and glanced past my shoulder across the rocky shore to the pines forty feet behind me. Maybe emboldened by what she didn't see there, I thought later, she leaned in. I smelled her soap-scrubbed skin when she kissed me on the lips.

The world didn't end, but everything except Loyalsock Creek paused. The spell broke when she turned and scampered like a startled doe across the rocks and into the trees to where her family must have been waiting in their car.

"Bye!" she shouted, her voice thrown back over her shoulder with her golden hair. The creek-side pines absorbed her.

Things like this don't happen to thirteen-year-old boys, except in our erotic imaginings. That soft kiss morphed over time to a Hollywood-length, sensual soul mingling, and now, all these years later, back to the sweet, fleeting peck it really was. For just a moment a veil had parted to a world I wasn't ready for. It didn't completely close.

For a while I stood, immobile, my heart and breathing slowing gradually to pedestrian rates, before I stooped to pick up a perfect stone and skimmed it hard across the face of the water in one motion. For the first time in thousands of throws, the rock skipped the full width of the creek and stopped against the other side with an abrupt granite-to-granite *crack!*

I was so light, I could have floated into the pine-scented air and ridden the wind right then. Maybe that's how Adam felt when his world was new.

UP A TREE

The world was flat where I grew up.

Levittown, Long Island, sits on seven square miles of the Hempstead Plains. Elevation above sea level varies only twenty feet or so over the whole town. No hills. For a Levittown kid, the best way to get up in the world was to climb a tree.

Tree climbing is a phase of childhood development. Everyone I knew, girls and boys alike, did it. For some, like me, the phase lasted years; for others, just one scary experience. But at some point, we all climbed.

The neighborhood kids called the strip of trees and brush between Loring Road and Wantagh Parkway "the woods." There, many climbable oaks and maples invited adventure. When we were old enough to scamper across Loring Road, we climbed training trees with easy-to-grasp lower branches. As legs and arms grew longer and stronger, so grew the size of trees we'd venture up.

I was not as fearless a climber as some of my friends. I once got myself pretty high in an old, gnarly maple and feared I couldn't get down. The hand- and footholds I'd used to ascend were no longer apparent when I looked for them, and the ground was frighteningly far below. My knees shook and I shifted my weight, afraid to step down to a limb I couldn't reach without commitment. My better-climber friends were already on the ground.

Colin shouted up at me, "Come on! Let's get going."

He didn't know I was frozen, hands close to cramping from holding on tightly to the branches my life depended on.

Colin and the other boys were eager to look for garter snakes. Tree climbing was a diversion.

"Go on. I'll catch up," I said, loudly, in as normal a voice as I could.

"Whatsamattah, you stuck?" Joel came back.

"Hey, Jack's scared to come down!" the grinning, crew-cut Colin announced to the others.

I couldn't bear the taunts and belittlement I knew would come next. The impending shame of being called a chicken by my friends was enough to push fear to arm's length. I took the impossible step down. My sneaker touched and caught, and the branch held. The rest of the way was okay; I dropped the last eight feet to the ground.

I was shaking inside, but they'd already forgotten and were rummaging through the brush, turning over rocks and pieces of trash, looking for snakes.

My boyhood buddy Ricky and I liked to climb the sycamore on the Loring Road edge of the McLaren Field grounds near his house. We called it the Ballpark Tree. It's still there, a towering specimen. It was taller than a Levitt house even back then, but easy to climb once we got into its first crotch of massive limbs. The trick was to reach that starting place. If I gave Ricky a boost, or he me, one of us could climb, but the other remained grounded. So we'd lean a bicycle against the trunk, stand on the seat to reach the first limb, and then clamber up. One summer somebody nailed short two-by-fours to the trunk to form a ladder anyone could climb.

The fruits of American sycamores are one-inch balls which hang on stalks. They start out green and turn brown in autumn. Around the time a new school year started, the ground beneath the Ballpark Tree would be littered with them, though a few stayed on the tree through winter. I've read that some people call them "buttonballs," but for reasons now lost, Ricky and I called them "archieballs." The Ballpark Tree was as solid as a building, and its rounded limbs were comfortable to hang out in for hours. I liked feeling embraced in its leafy canopy, safe to daydream unnoticed.

Trees have been around since the Garden of Eden. They symbolize the connection between earth and heaven, form and spirit. It's said their roots represent our pasts, the sturdy trunk and limbs our present, and the upper branches and leaves, our gifts and our potential. Trees feed off the sun's energy. They move oceans of pure water from the ground into the air, and receive it back again. Trees nourish the world. Is it any wonder people love them?

My parents bought a Levitt ranch-style house on the corner of Gun and Chimney Lanes in 1949, when I was two. A couple years later, Dad planted a tall, slender silver maple in our backyard. It was delivered by truck with its big root ball wrapped in brown burlap and tied with heavy rope. Our neighbor, Mr. Swain, and the truck driver helped Dad right it in the big hole and fill around it with dark dirt and peat moss.

The tree took to its new home right away, and shot up. By the time Ricky and I were big enough to climb it, it was big enough to be climbed. In ten years or so the silver maple was already one of the taller trees around—taller even than most of the older trees in the woods across Loring Road. It remained slender—much of its growth was *up*, not *out.* It was stately, nearly symmetrical, and its leaves fluttered in a breeze to flash their silvery-green undersides. Most importantly, it was easy to climb.

There came a time when the furthest notch I could reach in the silver maple allowed a viewpoint higher than the gabled rooflines of the surrounding houses. I could see Wisdom Lane School, and all the way north to some of the bigger buildings on Hempstead Turnpike. To the east the steeple of the Levittown Presbyterian Church on Wantagh Avenue stood out. However, I never learned to be fully at ease with the way my stomach fluttered when the tree swayed.

I could see into neighbors' yards and spy on them, but no one ever looked up to see me unless I yelled to them. The silver maple provided a secret hiding place in plain sight, a bark-and-leaf throne overlooking the world. I loved that tree. In my early teen years it was my vertical refuge. I could get away from everything without going anywhere but up. It was my haven of solitude.

Once, and just once, I stood in a notch as high in the silver maple as I dared. As ever, I felt like the Lord of Levittown in my high perch. However, this time, this once, was different. I felt the tree's *aliveness* as never before or after. This time I wasn't just a climber, a foreign visitor in the tree. I felt my legs and feet stretch all the way down the trunk and my toes spread into the earth. My head and shoulders extended upward into the air beyond the topmost leaf. I was *in* the tree, yes, but I felt the whole tree *in me.*

At peace in that leafy cathedral, I found myself enveloped in reverence for life. I was filled with it. I knew even then this was *big*—light years past my boyhood wonderment at nature's designs. My awareness flew open. Inside merged with outside. I *knew* the tree. For that time—a moment, a minute, an hour?—the tree and I were one thing, one life. I was surprised by joy.

I don't remember climbing the silver maple again after that inexplicable experience. I guess I didn't need to. Out of one clear, extraordinary event came a sense of kinship with life in everything. It has remained in me since.

When I last saw it, the silver maple had grown to dominate the small backyard and could be seen for blocks around. In the mid-1970s my parents sold their house in Levittown and moved to California. A subsequent owner hacked the maple down to make room for an in-ground swimming pool. I heard he built the pool without a permit and to questionable standards, and local authorities forced him to demolish it. A scar was left on the ground, only slowly healed over by new grass.

It was a grown-up Ricky who later told me of the maple's demise. It was sad news, of course, like the passing of a friend.

But axes don't fell family trees, and there's life beyond bark, limb, and leaf. In that silver maple I touched my tree of life.

We have always held to the hope, the belief, the conviction that there is a better life, a better world, beyond the horizon.

—Franklin Delano Roosevelt

Martha

A Short Story

The elderly woman seemed to misplace her mind now and then. It disconcerted her at first, but these days, when she didn't find it right away, she was content to wait. There was always a lot to look at. She'd watch the sky through her window, feeling connected with clouds as they cruised and morphed against the broad blue Midwest firmament. She'd admire sunlight illuminating a swath of her area rug, enlivening its colors to dance for her.

After a while, her mind would tire of whatever it had gone off to do, and come back. She'd remember her name: Martha. She'd remember Lincoln Senior Care, and that she was in her room here because she had nowhere else. She'd become aware again of her wheelchair, and the bend of her knees, the left one unfeeling since the stroke. She knew she never really lost her mind; it just went wandering without her. They were peaceful, these times that it left her here alone.

Martha adored the large lithograph on the ecru wall opposite her bed: a verdant rural scene of old oaks and elms framing a steeply rising meadow where two young girls in summer dresses played. They stood near each other, one looking intently at a lavender flower, the other smiling at a yellow butterfly on her finger. Up to the left, well beyond the girls, the rounded edge of the rise touched clear sky, and vanished.

An impressionist had painted the original. Details were largely left for observers to fill in as they enjoyed the picture's hues and imagined its stories. To Martha, the girls, the trees, the sloping meadow rich with greens, browns, and bright dabs of wildflowers seemed more lifelike than a photograph. She could hear the children's giggly voices and at times eavesdropped on their girl talk.

Her daughter Shelley had given Martha the print many birthdays ago. Remembering she'd outlived her daughter always brought a deep, cold ache in the pit of her stomach. Just after Christmas, her daughter's healthy forty-one-year-old heart had arrested after a ski run at Jackson Hole, and paramedics couldn't revive her. Twenty-two years had passed since then, but Martha no longer remembered that. She could relive the phone call as if she had just hung up.

"Celebrating, laughing one moment, then suddenly gone," Shelley's best friend had told Martha. She could still hear her voice. "We're in shock. I'm so sorry, Mrs. Watkins. How...? *Why?*"

A raging wolf could not have savaged Martha more than the news of Shelley's death. Every time the memory returned, Martha sat for a long time with her own questions, unmoving, her good side as paralyzed as her left.

Her days ran together. Martha would sit by her window when the weather was sunny and whenever snow had freshly whitened the scene outside. TV held no interest, and reading required too much effort anymore. The hours and days spent in the meadow with the girls in the lithograph were her pleasure. She would commune there, not even needing her eyes open to see the grasses and delicate wildflowers undulate in gentle puffs of breeze. A nurse might look in and think she was asleep or daydreaming, and not disturb her. Martha liked that.

The staff at Lincoln regularly prodded and poked her, moved her and fed her and changed her and washed her, and were generally kind to her. They'd smile and speak short phrases like "Good morning!" and "How are you today, Martha?" and "Lunch time." She would hear their dueling staccato voices from the hall outside her room, but making no sense of Spanish or Tagalog she had long since stopped paying attention. Once she heard Dr. James from beyond her open door say, "Martha Watkins, ninety-one: ischemic stroke, dementia," to whomever he was touring around.

They must think I'm deaf, too, she thought.

Martha liked playing dead. She could enjoy long stretches of uninterrupted time sitting perfectly still in her chair, eyes closed, lips forming a faint smile. Nobody knew she'd slipped into the meadow again.

But a touch on her shoulder would call her back. "Snack time, Martha."

She wasn't fond of the thick, chalky liquid, but obediently took little sips. She preferred black coffee, but didn't enjoy watching her pale, blue-veined and spotted hand tremble as it worked to hold the cup steady. Food was okay, but not important. Martha did as asked, taking a few bites of soft carrots or chicken or tapioca, but she'd soon turn back to the window or to the picture.

On a gray winter's afternoon the Shelley-news-phone-call was playing again in Martha's mind, and the familiar pain engulfed her. She could switch it off only by playing dead and escaping into the lithograph. This time it was exceptionally easy.

A nurse touched her. Then gently shook her. Martha didn't stir.

This time she didn't have to go back. White fog rolled into her room at Lincoln Senior Care. Martha turned her back on it, waved to the sunlit girls, and walked, then pranced, on well-toned legs, up the sloping meadow toward the clear sky beyond the trees. She felt as light as a woman in love again. For a long time she'd known something extraordinary awaited her just over the rise ahead, and she'd be there soon.

Epilogue

Writing stories about real people can open doors I didn't know were there.

Brad

"Brad" is a chapter from *Gift of Seeds,* my first book of memoir essays. The sleepy tractor ride I describe in it took place on my grandmother's Delaware farm sixty years ago. Yesterday, Brad phoned.

After my uncle Everett died in 1960, my grandmother leased her fields to other farmers, and Brad, my uncle's right-hand man, had to find work elsewhere. The last time I saw him was at my uncle's funeral. He stood to the side with his wife, Ivory. I hardly recognized him in a suit and without a sweat-stained cap.

In 2013, after *Gift of Seeds* was published, I sent an email to Uncle Everett's daughter, my cousin Mary Ann, in Milford, Delaware. I wrote her about the book and the people she knew who appear in it, including her father and our Grandma Stayton. Months later I received an email from Mary Ann's adult daughter, Stephanie. The email address I'd used is actually hers. Seems Mary Ann isn't much on email "but she'd love to talk," her daughter wrote back, and gave me the phone number.

We talked. We scarcely knew each other as children. Now, more than half a century later, we had our first real conversation. The next day she called me back and we talked some more. I was lucky to remember half the people she was bringing me up to date on.

A dust devil of details later, Mary Ann said, "Brad lives right here in Milford. I run into him once in a while."

"Do you have his address?" I asked.

Mary Ann looked up "Bradie Worthy" in a phone book. A younger person might not recognize the sound, but I heard her flipping the pages. The next morning I mailed Brad a letter with a copy of *Gift of Seeds*, intending to wait a week and then call him.

He called me first. Mary Ann had given him my number. My smarter-than-me phone already knew the call was from an unknown number in Milford, and I knew it had to be Brad.

"Jack? That you?"

His voice touched a gossamer wisp of memory, but this was an older, rural-sounding man, articulate, his tone gravelly but distantly familiar. He knew me by Jack, my childhood nickname.

"Brad!" I exclaimed.

"Yes it is! I got your book. Thank you! Thank you. I've never been so surprised. Nobody ever wrote such nice things about me. Brings me back to a finer time, a happy time... Your grandma and your uncle were good people, and real good to me..."

We exchanged niceties about family and friends, past and present.

"I read other stories in the book and liked them, but I keep going back to 'Brad' and reading it again. I'm still just soaking it up."

I had thanked Brad in my letter to him, saying the meaning and importance of that long-ago time have stayed with me and influenced how I've seen the world ever since.

"Please accept this *Gift of Seeds* with my profound gratitude for the positive, formative part you played in my upbringing," I'd inscribed in the book I sent him.

After a short silence, Brad said, softly, "I had no idea, no idea... no idea at all..."

I could almost see him slowly shaking his gray-haired head in time with the words he dropped one by one into the phone. Feelings arose from a deep well of a time long gone. His voice trembled. I teared up too.

Neither of us had had any idea, until then.

Rona's Closet

I'm glad Rona realized I was never in her closet. I feel relieved to no longer be thought guilty of something I didn't do. There were plenty of things I *did* do. I don't need any extras.

At the fiftieth-year reunion of the Levittown Memorial High School graduating class of 1965, Rona spoke with Colin and Joel, two of the three parties of closet infamy. None of us know where the third might be these days, a kid we knew back then as Ricky Murray. Rona reported that Joel recalls his part in the unsuccessful Pistachio Closet Caper, but when she mentioned it to Colin, he stared at her blankly.

I believe the ability to forget is just about as valuable as the ability to remember. Too bad we can't always choose. I bet Colin remembers our catching garter snakes in the woods along Loring Road, though.

Bernie

After I'd written a draft and a revision or two of "The Fresh Air Kid," buddy Ricky and his fellow cyber-sleuths Barbara and Terry McCarthy began searching for Bernie. Barbara followed the return address on the 1960 thank-you note Bernie had sent to Ricky's mother and found the Gowanus Apartments in Brooklyn, the development where Bernie's family lived the summer he spent those two weeks in Levittown. She discovered an Internet-posted article entitled "Gowanus Houses Old Timers Day" in which the deaths of Bernard Kinsey and his brother Horace are mentioned.

Barbara then located a moving obituary for Kinzé Bernard "Pop" Kinsey printed in the December 20–26, 2012, edition of *Our Time Press*, a local weekly. The article included a color photo of a smiling Bernie with gray stubble—almost a half-century older than the Bernie Ricky and I knew, but with the same laughing eyes. Clearly, "our" Bernie.

Some excerpts from the obituary, published without byline:

"Educated in the New York Public School System, 'Pop' graduated from the illustrious Boys High School in 1966. He became a staple of the Gowanus community as 'Pop the Bop,' a cool head with no enemies. This characteristic would move with him throughout life...

"Bernard 'Pop' Kinsey leaves a legacy as wide, deep, and expansive as the ocean's water. A Man. A Black Man. A Real Man. A Father. A Grandpop. A Son. A Brother through Blood and through Action. An active listener. A wise counselor. A man with a fashion sense [of his own]. A man with a sense of humor. A man of practical compassion. A man of sacrifice. A fair man... A lover of sports... An employee [who gave] his boss advice. An aficionado of jazz. A man who would open his home to thousands... A man with his own philosophy on everything. A grown man who tickled other grown people and children alike. An analyst of problems. A giver of solutions. A friend. A husband. An ancestor...

"Kinzé Bernard 'Pop' Kinsey was preceded in death by [three brothers]. He is survived by his mother, Mary Kinsey... his wife, Dr. Shadidi Beatrice Kinsey, his [six children], [seven grandchildren], and a host of nieces, nephews, cousins, aunts, uncles, extended family and friends who witnessed his greatness and know the world is better because he walked it."

We didn't find Bernie soon enough to talk with him in person, but it's apparent he lived his life in the quality of character we saw more than a hint of when he was a twelve-year-old Fresh Air kid in Levittown.

Levittown Essays

Hi, John,

My name is Sandy Fountain Gerson. I attended your book reading at the Levittown Historical Society Museum and purchased a copy of Gift of Seeds.

Thank you for giving me a wonderful new way to interact with my sister Bev. In 2003 while living in Brooklyn, she stepped off the sidewalk one morning to hail a cab near her apartment, and was hit by a car. Multiple injuries left her almost unrecognizable. Most severe was head trauma. Many surgeries and many bedside vigils and prayers later, she awoke after two months in a coma as a different person, but we still had her. Following a long hospital stay she has since been in a nursing home close to where I live. I visit her every week. Her short-term cognitive functions are permanently damaged, but by reading something or sharing an old movie with her I am often able to connect with her long-ago memory. She just loves your stories, John, especially the ones about Levittown. In those moments I have my sister back again. I am forever grateful! We have already read your book twice...

• • •

Thank you so much for sending me a [pre-publication] draft of "Bowling with Dad." I just visited Bev and read it to her. We loved it! It brought back some memories of our own dad. We were also a bowling family. My dad managed my Uncle Stan's Bowl Mart store in Mineola. Neither Bev nor I ever became even so-so bowlers ourselves, but bowling was a big part of our lives. Your story brought little-girl memories back...

•   •   •

Did I tell you the Ricky of your memoirs was the first boy I ever held hands with? My dad was pretty strict about boys at that age. Our short boyfriend/girlfriend time passed quickly at Bluegrass Lane Pool the summer of seventh grade. To this day I remember Ricky as a handsome, sweet boy who was always the gentleman...

•   •   •

Bev is older than me by eighteen months. We were so close in age our mom dressed us alike until we revolted in middle school. She was my very first special best friend.

She was fifty-six when the accident occurred. We've been told that with this type of brain trauma there is a marked increase in the likelihood of dementia developing. So far Bev still recognizes me. I am grateful every time I enter her room and she smiles and says, "Sandy."

•   •   •

We grew up on Barnyard Lane right in back of the Levittown Library, near Bluegrass Pool. Bev and I shared a bedroom until I was thirteen. All those years we would confide our adventures and dreams and just about everything two girls could share—even our clothes when we were old enough to have different outfits.

Dementia works backwards from the present in that current memories fade quickly and older ones linger. For us, our Levittown memories are in the forefront of our relationship. When I sit on her bed and we read your stories we are once again two young sisters laughing and sharing like we did in that small Levitt bedroom. It is the last unbroken connection we have, and I treasure every shared memory and moment your stories evoke.

I don't know how long she will be able to recall even these memories, so our moments together are all the more poignant and treasured. We are both truly grateful.

Your Levittown Fans,
Sandy and Bev

Tied Ends
The real Bob of "Kansas Bob" from *Gift of Seeds* wrote me a letter in care of my publisher in 2013. Someone had told him of the book and he'd gotten a copy. He said he had no objection to the way I'd portrayed him in the essay, but, typical of Bob, he wrote a humorously edgy justification of his idiosyncrasies. I sent an appreciative missive back to him at his Olathe address. I would have enjoyed but didn't expect an ongoing correspondence, and it didn't happen. I later learned Kansas Bob died suddenly a few months later. I'm glad we completed a circuit together before then.

• • •

A last reunion around Ellen's kitchen table of the "When Pigs Flew" friends is envisioned to coincide with the confluence of three future events: her retirement, the sale of the family house on Target Lane, and her moving from Levittown. These could all happen in 2016, or maybe in 2017 or 2018, or even later. No matter how practical the change, it's not easy to uproot.

The friends who reminisced at Ellen's circular table that day have some roots there too. We'd all spent innumerable hours around Ellen's parents' round table during our adolescent years and beyond. It was a common point of our growing up until, one by one, we spun off into our larger lives.

• • •

This small group of mostly former Levittowners wondered what had become of Jeffrey of "Fish Story." We'd all known one another as kids, but apparently, among us, I was the sole beneficiary, ever, of his mother's perfect tuna salad—other than Jeffrey himself, of course.

Doug and Karen checked out Jeffrey's old Gun Lane house and there found his sister, living alone. She told our inquirers she had not been in touch with Jeffrey in many, many years and knew nothing of him. Some old addresses lead nowhere.

• • •

My usual experience when revisiting someplace I knew well long ago is how changed it is now. Sometimes it's because *I've* changed: *Wait! The doorknobs in my grandmother's farmhouse were at eye level...* Sometimes things really *have* changed, like the hundreds of tract houses that replaced acres of citrus trees next to where we used to live near Corona, California.

Change is inexorable. It's comforting, however, to visit a place unseen for decades and find it the same. This was my experience at Pennsylvania's World's End State Park a few years ago. The essay "World's End" began gurgling up from a deep source when I stood on Loyalsock Creek's same rocky shore where I'd spent boyhood hours skipping stones. Only the passing water itself is new; everything else was and is as I remember it. I picked up a small, flat stone and flung it hard, sidearm, across the water's surface. It skipped six times and stopped against a boulder on the opposite bank with a satisfying *crack!* The sound triggered the memories that eventually transmuted into the essay.

Loma
Every essay and story in this book and in *Gift of Seeds* attended finishing school in Wisconsin. There they brushed up on grammar and syntax, had storyline subluxations adjusted, their sentence structures and word choices tactfully questioned, and their tenses tweaked. A few were even expelled by mutual agreement. The worthy ones flew back and forth via email as many as a dozen times before my editor, Loma Huh, and I finally deemed them "semi-final." Even then they were aged in a holding file before a final pre-publication review. Only then were they ready for your eyes.

Loma is a freelance professional editor. Though I never see her in person, she's a friend. She's raised her two children on her own, supported a home and a life in a small Wisconsin town I've never seen except via Google Earth. I pay her normal rate, but Loma and I have an understanding that her "real" work from big publishers with high-pressure deadlines has priority over mine. What she could probably do in a week of concentrated attention, we spread over a few months. It's a relaxed, enjoyable pace, and I feel it gives each essay and story time to ripen.

Some writers grumble and have little good to say about their editors. I have only the highest praise for Loma. Each essay and story she touches returns home refined, confident, and poised for its debut.

ACKNOWLEDGMENTS

First and always, to Pamela.

To Richard McCool, aka Ricardo McFresco as well as more secret pseudonyms, for his immeasurable memory assistance on Levittown stories. Ricardo's DNA is in many essays in both *If I Die Thursday* and its predecessor, *Gift of Seeds*.

To Amanda Woloshyn, computer graphic artist extraordinaire, for her technical skill and pixel magic on the cover and internal images.

To lifelong friend Ellen Smiley, owner of the round kitchen table on Target Lane, Levittown.

To Bill Gronenthal and Doug Turner, round-table accomplices in "When Pigs Flew."

To Sandy and Peter Jensen, lingual and literary mavens both, for invaluable enthusiasm, encouragement, and kind critiques.

To the late Martin Cecil for transcendent inspiration.

To my Orange County, California, writers' critique group: Janet Simcic, Dennis Phinney, Brenda Barrie, M. J. Buist, Denise Longrie, and Ana Arrelano, for hours of patient listening and innumerable insights and astute suggestions.

To Loma Huh, best editor west of Lake Michigan.

To the late Jim Wellemeyer for forty-five years' fine friendship and his example to many of a life well lived.

To Cliff and Kathy Penwell, forever friends who live where writing comes from.

To my son, Broc Gray, for creative ideas later born as "Soliloquy."

To Peggy Gretsch, for the "alphabet song" graphic and her eternal wit.

To Judy Weissman, my sister, for her long-ago makeup artistry that made me a she in "Once a Girl."

To Alan Hammond, who said he's glad I didn't die that Thursday or any Thursday since.

To Google Search for finding obscure stuff and to Google Earth for flying me all over for free.

To my brother, David Gray, for much more than he knows, but this time for his research and assistance with "Bowling with Dad."

To Andy Weissman, my brother-in-law and a real rodeo bulldogger, for his technical help with "All Around Cowboy" and for the photo of himself to accompany it.

To David Washington, one who knows, for consultation on "The Fresh Air Kid."

And to many more friends for their support and encouragement, including Peter Anderson, Randyl Appel, Ilse and Joel Appel, David Barnes and Anne Blaney, Lee Biesiadecki, Vince and Jeanne Bond, Bernie and Linda Bramante, Mickey Brown, Malena Carrión, Dan Cartwright, Jeannie Crocker, Jim Crowner, Mary Ann Day, Ceci Enciso y Ricardo Garcia, Joe Enzweiler and Todd Hunter, Mia Euvard, Anne Fees, Steve and Karen Frankel, Frank Frazier, Sandy Gerson, Karla Gervais, Louise Hanlon, Allan and Dianne Herauf, Ed Kauffman, Larry and Joyce Krantz, Dawn Kuykendall, Levittown Historical Society, Dan Liniger, Flo and Dave Liniger, Sandra Lopez, Rupert Maskell, Denise Matis, Barbara and Terry McCarthy, Jennifer Merrett, Linda Milks, Debbi Mingus, Todd and Susan Montgomery, Terry and Kathryn Oftedal, Wes Phillips, Agustín Resendiz, Lou and Bridget Rotola, Eduardo Saad, Rona Selsky, Luanne Somers, Debra Stein, Linda Stewart, Pamela Tallman, Carol Travis, and Gail Wagner.

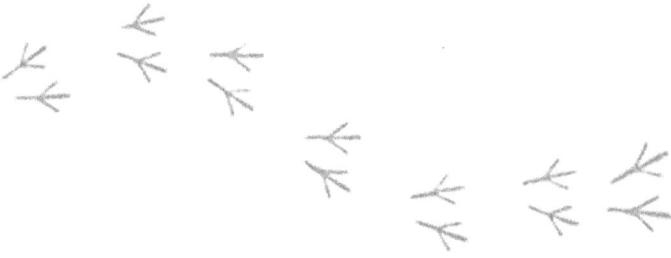

About the Author
John Clinton Gray

After childhood in Levittown, New York, and college in Cincinnati, Ohio, John's first career as an engineer made it clear he was better with words and people than with numbers and things. John and his wife, Pamela, met and married in Colorado, lived in Arizona, then moved to southern California where they founded and, for decades, led a spiritual community and one of the most successful spa businesses in America. They raised their family and traveled extensively, John as a public speaker and, recently, as a writer. John and Pamela have two grown children, two grandchildren, and are happily empty-nesting near Lake Elsinore, California.

www.ingramcontent.com/pod-product-compliance
Lightning Source LLC
LaVergne TN
LVHW011218080426
835509LV00005B/187